Richard Swan

Series Editor: Marian Cox

The Pardoner's Prologue & Tale

Geoffrey Chaucer

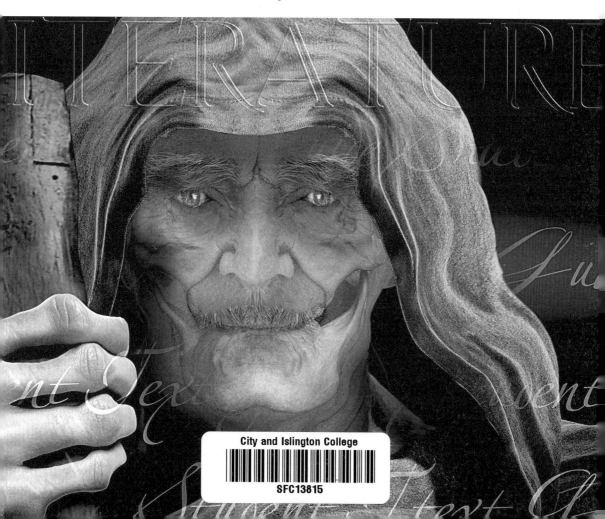

City and Islington College

SFC13815

Philip Allan Updates, an imprint of Hodder Education, an Hachette UK company, Market Place, Deddington, Oxfordshire OX15 0SE

Orders
Bookpoint Ltd, 130 Milton Park, Abingdon, Oxfordshire, OX14 4SB
tel: 01235 827720
fax: 01235 400454
e-mail: uk.orders@bookpoint.co.uk
Lines are open 9.00 a.m.–5.00 p.m., Monday to Saturday, with a 24-hour message answering service. You can also order through the Philip Allan Updates website: www.philipallan.co.uk

© Philip Allan Updates 2009

ISBN 978-0-340-97442-1

First printed 2009

Impression number   5   4   3   2   1

Year   2014   2013   2012   2011   2010   2009

CITY AND ISLINGTON
SIXTH FORM COLLEGE
283 - 309 GOSWELL ROAD
LONDON
EC1
TEL 020 7520 0652

All rights reserved; no part of this publication may be reproduced, stored in a retrieval system, or transmitted, in any form or by any means, electronic, mechanical, photo-copying, recording or otherwise without either the prior written permission of Philip Allan Updates or a licence permitting restricted copying in the United Kingdom issued by the Copyright Licensing Agency Ltd, Saffron House, 6–10 Kirby Street, London EC1N 8TS.

In all cases we have attempted to trace and credit copyright owners of material used.

Printed in Malta

Environmental information
Hachette UK's policy is to use papers that are natural, renewable and recyclable products and made from wood grown in sustainable forests. The logging and manufacturing processes are expected to conform to the environmental regulations of the country of origin.

P01434

8.99

SFC13815

Contents

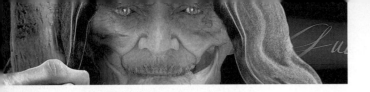

Introduction

Aims of the guide

The purpose of this Student Text Guide to 'The Pardoner's Prologue and Tale' is to enable you to organise your thoughts and responses to the text, to deepen your understanding of key features and aspects, and finally to help you to address the particular requirements of examination questions in order to obtain the best possible grade. The guide contains a number of summaries, lists, analyses and references to help with the content and construction of essay assignments. References to the text are to the Cambridge University Press edition, edited by A. C. Spearing.

It is assumed that you have read and studied the text already under the guidance of a teacher or lecturer. This is a revision guide, not an introduction, although some of its content serves the purpose of providing initial background. It can be read in its entirety in sequence, or it can be dipped into and used as a reference guide to specific and separate aspects of the text.

The remainder of this *Introduction* section consists of: Assessment Objectives; a revision scheme that gives a suggested programme for using the material in the guide; and practical advice on writing essay answers.

The *Text Guidance* section consists of a series of subsections that examine key aspects of the text including contexts, interpretations and controversies. Emboldened terms within this section are glossed in 'literary terms and concepts' on pp. 74–77.

The final section, *Questions and Answers*, includes sample essay question material and a guide to resources for further study.

Assessment Objectives

The revised AOs for A-level English Literature are common to all boards:

AO1	Articulate creative, informed and relevant responses to literary texts, using appropriate terminology and concepts, and coherent, accurate written expression.
AO2	Demonstrate detailed critical understanding in analysing the ways in which structure, form and language shape meanings in literary texts.
AO3	Explore connections and comparisons between different literary texts, informed by interpretations of other readers.
AO4	Demonstrate understanding of the significance and influence of the contexts in which literary texts are written and received.

Revision advice

For the examined units it is possible that either brief or more extensive revision will be necessary because the original study of the text took place some time previously. It is therefore useful to know how to go about revising and which tried and tested methods are considered the most successful for literature exams at all levels, from GCSE to degree finals.

Below is a guide on how *not* to do it — think of reasons why not in each case.

Don't:

- leave it until the last minute
- assume you remember the text well enough and don't need to revise at all
- spend hours designing a beautiful revision schedule
- revise more than one text at the same time
- think you don't need to revise because it is an open book exam
- decide in advance what you think the questions will be and revise only for those
- try to memorise particular essay plans
- reread texts randomly and aimlessly
- revise for longer than two hours in one sitting
- miss school lessons in order to work alone at home
- try to learn a whole ring-binder's worth of work
- rely on a study guide instead of the text

There are no short cuts to effective exam revision; the only way to know a text well, and to know your way around it in an exam, is to have done the necessary studying. If you use the following method, in six easy stages, for both open and closed book revision, you will not only revisit and reassess all your previous work on the text in a manageable way but will be able to distil, organise and retain your knowledge. Don't try to do it all in one go: take regular breaks for refreshment and a change of scene.

(1) Between a month and a fortnight before the exam, depending on your schedule (a simple list of stages with dates displayed in your room, not a work of art!), you will need to reread the text, this time taking stock of all the underlinings and marginal annotations as well. As you read, collect onto sheets of A4 the essential ideas and quotations as you come across them. The acts of selecting key material and recording it as notes are natural ways of stimulating thought and aiding memory.

(2) Reread the highlighted areas and marginal annotations in your critical extracts and background handouts, and add anything useful from them to your list of notes and quotations. Then reread your previous essays and the teacher's comments. As you look back through essays written earlier in the course, you should have the pleasant sensation of realising that you can now write much better on the text than

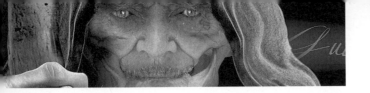

you could then. You will also discover that much of your huge file of notes is redundant or repeated, and that you have changed your mind about some beliefs, so that the distillation process is not too daunting. Selecting what is important is the way to crystallise your knowledge and understanding.

(3) During the run-up to the exam you need to do lots of practice essay plans to help you identify any gaps in your knowledge and give you practice in planning in five to eight minutes. Past paper titles for you to plan are provided in this guide, some of which can be done as full timed essays — and marked strictly according to exam criteria — which will show whether length and timing are problematic for you. If you have not seen a copy of a real exam paper before you take your first module, ask to see a past paper so that you are familiar with the layout and rubric.

(4) About a week before the exam, reduce your two or three sides of A4 notes to a double-sided postcard of very small, dense writing. Collect a group of keywords by once again selecting and condensing, and use abbreviations for quotations (first and last word), and character and place names (initials). (For the comparison unit your postcard will need to refer to key points, themes and quotations in both texts relevant to the specific theme or genre topic.) The act of choosing and writing out the short quotations will help you to focus on the essential issues, and to recall them quickly in the exam. Make sure that your selection covers the main themes and includes examples of symbolism, style, comments on character, examples of irony, point of view or other significant aspects of the text. Previous class discussion and essay writing will have indicated which quotations are useful for almost any title; pick those which can serve more than one purpose, for instance those that reveal character and theme, and are also an example of language. In this way a minimum number of quotations can have maximum application.

(5) You now have in a compact, accessible form all the material for any possible essay title. There are only half a dozen themes relevant to a literary text, so if you have covered these, you should not meet with any nasty surprises when you read the exam questions. You don't need to refer to your file of paperwork again, or even to the text. For the few days before the exam, you can read through your handy postcard whenever and wherever you get the opportunity. Each time you read it, which will only take a few minutes, you are reminding yourself of all the information you will be able to recall in the exam to adapt to the general title or to support an analysis of particular passages.

(6) A fresh, active mind works wonders, and information needs time to settle, so don't try to cram just before the exam. Relax the night before and get a good night's sleep. Then you will be able to enter the exam room with all the confidence of a well-prepared candidate.

Writing examination essays

Exam essays

In studying Chaucer for the examination, you need to know which Assessment Objectives are being tested and where the heaviest weighting falls, as well as whether it is a closed or clean text exam. You will probably have looked at or practised past paper questions so that you know what kind of title to expect, and it would be helpful if your teacher discussed the examiners' reports for previous years' exams with you.

Close reference to text is required even in closed text exams, and as quotation demonstrates 'use of text' it is often the most concise way of supporting a point. Exam essays should be clearly structured, briskly argued, concisely expressed, closely focused, and supported by brief but constant textual references. They should show a combination of familiarity, understanding, analytical skill and informed personal response. Length is not in itself an issue — quality matters rather than quantity — but you have to prove your knowledge and fulfil the assessment criteria, and without sufficient coverage and exploration of the title you cannot be awarded a top mark. Aim to write approximately 12 paragraphs or three to four sides of A4.

Do not take up one absolute position and argue only one interpretation. There are no 'yes' or 'no' answers in literature. Consider alternative views before deciding which one to argue, and mention the others first to prove your awareness of different reader opinions. It is permissible to say your response is equally balanced, provided that you have explained the contradictory evidence and proved that ambivalence is built into the text.

It is a useful class activity to play at being examiners and to set essay titles in groups and exchange them for planning practice. This makes you think about the main issues. Try to get into the way of thinking like an examiner and using their kind of language for expressing titles, which must avoid vagueness and ambiguity.

Exam essay process

The secret of exam essay success is a good plan, which covers and explores the title and refers to the four elements of text: plot, characterisation, language and themes. Think about the issues afresh rather than attempting to regurgitate your own or someone else's ideas, and avoid giving the impression of a pre-packaged essay that you are determined to deliver whatever the title.

- When you have chosen a question, underline its key words and define them briefly, in as many ways as are relevant to the text, to form the introduction and provide the background. Plan the rest of the essay, staying focused on the question, in approximately 12 points, recorded as short phrases with indication of support. Include a concluding point that does not repeat anything already said

but that pulls your ideas together to form an overview. It may refer to other readers' opinions, refer back to the title, or include a relevant quotation from the text or elsewhere.

- Check your plan to see that you have dealt with all parts of the question, have used examples of the four elements of text in your support, and have analysed, not just described. Remind yourself of the Assessment Objectives (printed on the exam paper). Group points and organise the plan into a structure with numbers, brackets or arrows.

- Tick off the points in your plan as you use them in the writing of your essay, and put a diagonal line through the whole plan once you have finished. You can add extra material as you write, as long as it does not take you away from the outline you have constructed. Concentrate on expressing yourself clearly as you write your essay, and on writing accurately, concisely and precisely. Integrate short quotations throughout the essay.

- Allow five minutes at the end for checking and improving your essay in content and style. Insertions and crossings-out, if legible, are encouraged. As well as checking accuracy of spelling, grammar and punctuation, watch out for errors of fact, name or title slips, repetition, and absence of linkage between paragraphs. Make sure your conclusion sounds conclusive, and not as though you have run out of time, ink or ideas. A few minutes spent checking can make the difference of a grade.

Planning practice

Using some of the titles from the *Questions and Answers* section, which are based on the draft specifications of the different exam boards, practise writing essay plans within a time limit of eight minutes, using about half a page. Aim for at least ten points and know how you would support them. Use numbers to structure your plan. Do this in groups and exchange and compare plans. Get used to using note form and abbreviations for names to save time, and to not using your text. Even in an open text exam, the best-performing students rarely use their text.

Since beginnings are the most daunting part of an essay for many students, you could also practise writing opening paragraphs for your planned essays. Remember to define the terms of the title, especially any abstract words. This will give your essay breadth, depth and structure (e.g. if the word 'morality' appears, say exactly what you take 'morality' to mean, and how many different things it can mean in the context of the text).

Students also find conclusions difficult, so experiment with writing final paragraphs for the essays you have planned. The whole essay is working towards the conclusion, so you need to know what it is going to be before you start writing the essay, and to make it clear that you have proved your case, whatever that may be.

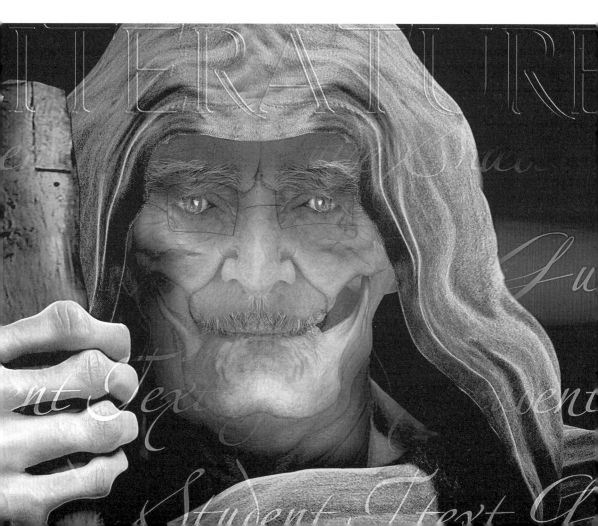

Text Guidance

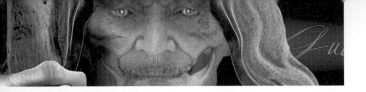

Contexts

The medieval context

The medieval worldview

The worldview that would have been shared by Chaucer and his European contemporaries was markedly different from that of today, and you need to gain an understanding of it if you are to make proper sense of Chaucer's writings. Much of the information that follows was innate knowledge for any medieval person, and so explicit references to it rarely occur.

The physical universe

The universe had been created by God, and was finite, comprehensible and purposeful; it existed as a home for man. Every element could be explained and every element was interrelated, so that the place and functioning of one aspect of the universe could be understood within the operation of the whole structure.

The Ptolemaic system

The cosmological model accepted in the medieval period is known as the Ptolemaic system, being a refinement of the ideas propounded by the Egyptian astronomer Ptolemy in the second century AD. This model held sway for well over 1,000 years, and was only superseded by more modern models based on the Copernican system long after the end of the Middle Ages.

According to the Ptolemaic system, the universe consisted of nine concentric transparent crystal spheres, with the Earth at the centre. Each of the first seven spheres contained a planet: in order, the Moon, Mercury, Venus, the Sun, Mars, Jupiter and Saturn. The eighth sphere contained the fixed stars. The ninth sphere, the so-called *primum mobile* (prime mover), contained no planet of its own, but its motion imparted movement to all the other spheres. God, who existed outside the created universe, controlled the whole process. The universe was therefore thought to be a clock-like mechanism, and the sound made by the mechanism could be imagined, or in certain exceptional circumstances heard. This was the famed 'music of the spheres', a divine harmony that inspired many writers, artists and musicians.

Heaven was thought to be the area outside the created universe, which yields the idea of going 'up' to heaven. Heaven itself was unaffected by time, movement or change. Between the *primum mobile* and the Moon there was movement but no decay or change; everything was perfect and divine. Change was limited to events within the sphere of the Moon, and therefore on Earth. This explained weather systems, the atmosphere, and the whole idea of human life being sub-lunar — literally, below the Moon. Events on Earth were affected by the movement of all the spheres — hence belief in astrology — but events taking place on Earth itself only affected the universe as far as the Moon. The deaths of Julius Caesar and King Duncan in Shakespeare's plays, for example, therefore cause chaos in the natural world and in the skies. The Moon, being the closest planet to Earth, had the most influence on human affairs, which explains why 'lunatics' were thought of as being directly affected by the Moon. Hell, rather neatly, found its place at the centre of the Earth, simultaneously suggesting the idea of going 'down' to Hell and meaning that Hell was at the furthest possible remove from Heaven.

The Great Chain of Being

Parallel to the physical order in the structure of the universe was the logical order implied by the medieval belief in hierarchy. The system by which everything on Earth was believed to be organised is generally known as the Great Chain of Being. This categorised all of the items in the universe, with God at the top and inanimate matter at the bottom. The table below shows this hierarchy and the associated properties of each item.

Item	Properties
God	Reason, Movement, Life, Existence
Angels	Reason, Movement, Life, Existence
Man	Reason, Movement, Life, Existence
Animals	Movement, Life, Existence
Plants	Life, Existence
Inanimate matter	Existence

The hierarchy was governed by the universal principle that it is the duty of each creature to obey those higher up the hierarchy, and the responsibility of each creature to govern those below it. This gives rise to some important observations. First, it is the duty of all creatures to obey God. Equally, it is God's duty to govern his universe responsibly. Mankind was created 'in God's image', which means possessing the same attributes; it is the faculty of reason that sets humans apart from all other creatures on Earth. It is the duty of mankind to obey God and the messages conveyed by his angels; it is the responsibility of mankind to govern the Earth in accordance with God's wishes.

As with the universe itself, once this system is understood a large number of things make sense. The Fall of Man, the original sin when Adam and Eve disobeyed God (symbolically by eating an apple), entailed a fundamental violation of the Great Chain of Being, and it is no surprise that its consequences were therefore absolute. Genesis makes clear that their sin was to disrupt the hierarchy by believing themselves to be higher than they were — they fell prey to the devil's temptation that they would be 'as Gods, knowing good and evil'. Satan himself fell from heaven because of the same sin of pride, believing himself equal to God when his duty was

to obey his natural superior. In the opposite direction, a medieval person would utterly condemn animal rights supporters for failure to understand the hierarchy. Over the last few centuries this sense of vertical hierarchy has been dismantled, so that many people no longer recognise a deity that is 'above' them, and equally refuse to claim superiority over creatures notionally 'below' them.

Hierarchies within the groups

Within each part of the hierarchy, further hierarchies existed, giving rise to the concept of 'degree' — one's exact positioning on the social scale. There was a hierarchy within the animals, which is why the lion is still often referred to as the 'king' of the beasts. Among human beings, several such hierarchies were visible. In secular society, the king was the sole ruler, followed by the nobility (themselves with several ranks) and then the rest; even among the peasants there were various gradings depending on their conditions of service or tenure. The parallel structure in the Church had the pope as the supreme authority, and a number of ranks from cardinal, archbishop and bishop down to parish priest and curate. In every case the same governing rule applied, which is why kings and popes could claim divine sanction for their rule and why regicide was viewed with such horror.

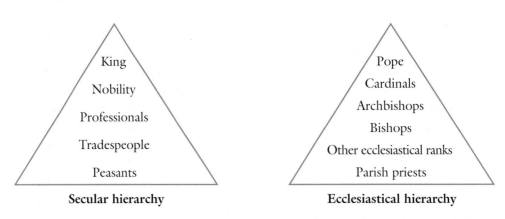

Secular hierarchy   **Ecclesiastical hierarchy**

The tension between the two hierarchies caused problems, most famously in the case of Thomas Becket. A friend and chancellor to Henry II, Becket was appointed by the king as Archbishop of Canterbury. Henry hoped that this would give him power over the Church, but Becket defied him and claimed that ecclesiastical authority was higher than secular authority. This led to Becket's assassination in 1170, and the start of the veneration of him as a saint that made Canterbury the leading pilgrimage site in England.

The final significant hierarchical distinction, and the one with the most far-reaching implications for Western society and history, was the claim that men were hierarchically superior to women, a doctrine founded on Genesis. This meant that men could and should rule over women, and women had to obey their husbands.

Until recently, the standard Christian marriage service included the vow that the wife would obey the husband, but without the reciprocal promise of obedience from the man. Centuries of institutionalised inequality and anti-feminism were an automatic concomitant of such a belief, the repercussions of which are still felt today.

However, despite this notion of the relative status of men and women, the situation in reality was always more complex. Debate over the relative status, rights and responsibilities of men and women was as rife in Chaucer's time as it is today. There was a large corpus of antifeminist writing because most writers were male clerics, but it is clear that women were far from silent, as Chaucer reveals in his portrayal of the Wife of Bath. Much of *The Canterbury Tales* is concerned with this topic, with all kinds of relationships and attitudes being portrayed.

Medieval society

The three estates model

Medieval society comprised three classes or estates: those who fought, those who prayed, and those who laboured to sustain the first two groups. In principle, this was the basis of feudal society.

The first estate was the clergy, a large group that maintained the fabric of society through the service of God and the regulation of human affairs. The second estate was the nobility, who were few in number, and were landowners and professional soldiers. The third estate was the vast bulk of ordinary people, who were subject to the laws of both the other groups. In a primarily agrarian society, this group comprised mainly peasants who laboured on the land to create the food and wealth by which society was sustained. A person was born into either the second or third estate, and might enter the first (the clergy) through vocation or for a variety of other reasons, including a desire for security or advancement. Otherwise, people were expected to remain in the rank to which God had allocated them at birth.

In addition to being members of one of the three estates, medieval women were also placed in three categories: virgin, wife and widow. They tended to be thought of as inferior in consequence and importance to men.

In practice, the structure of medieval society was not as simple as the three estates model suggests, and by Chaucer's lifetime significant changes had taken place. From the start, there were inequalities in the third estate, which necessarily covered a vast range of occupations. With the passing of time people strove to better their conditions, and by the fourteenth century there were numerous distortions and anomalies within the system. The range of characters in *The Canterbury Tales* illustrates this. The only members of the nobility are the Knight and his son the Squire. The only true peasant is the Ploughman. There are several members of the clergy, but only three women. The remaining pilgrims all occupy a shifting middle ground; they are technically members of the third estate, but to equate the Man of Law — a wealthy, influential professional — with the Miller is clearly absurd.

Although class distinctions continue to exist to this day, it is evident that the feudal division into classes had already lost much of its practical significance long before the end of the Middle Ages; *The Canterbury Tales* amply shows how there was a blurring of position, wealth and influence in this period.

Social change

The late fourteenth century was a time of great change, which makes *The Canterbury Tales* a valuable window onto an important period in English history.

The Black Death

The catalyst for change was the outbreak of the plague known as the Black Death. This swept through Europe and devastated England on several occasions in the fourteenth century, most radically in 1348–49, early in Chaucer's life. The exact figures are unknown, but estimates suggest that up to 40% of England's population died. The effects of this were colossal. Before the mid-fourteenth century, the population had been expanding, meaning that labour was plentiful and land use was intensive. Afterwards, labour became scarcer, but pressures on land decreased. Thousands of individual jobs and roles were lost. Inevitably, there was suddenly scope for enterprising people from all ranks of society to seek better conditions and better occupations.

The Peasants' Revolt

Social unrest was a likely outcome of social change, and it is not surprising that the uprising known as the Peasants' Revolt occurred in 1381. This rebellion was primarily triggered by increased taxation, and resulted in a march on the city of London and demands for the eradication of serfdom. The rebellion gained little of immediate consequence, but it offers an important insight into the way that society was changing at a rapid pace. At the time, Chaucer was living above Aldgate, one of the six city gates of London, so he must have had an intimate awareness of the events that took place.

Language

Further changes were probably hastened by the upheaval following the outbreaks of plague. It was during Chaucer's lifetime that English re-emerged as the official language of court and the law, supplanting the Norman French that William the Conqueror had imposed and paving the way for the dominance of what would become Modern English in the nation and beyond. This is reflected in Chaucer's choice of English for all his major works; by comparison, his friend John Gower wrote three major works, one in English, one in French and one in Latin.

The Church

Although it remained a paramount power both in politics and in society, the Church was also subject to upheaval at this time. In 1378, one of the years in which Chaucer visited Italy, the Great Schism took place. This was a rift in the Church which resulted in the election of two popes — an unimaginable situation if one considers the hierarchical significance of the pope as the appointed representative of God on Earth. The Italians had elected Urban VI as pope, but the French, supported by their king, Charles V, appointed Clement VII, who set up his throne in Avignon. Like the Peasants' Revolt, the Great Schism led to further questioning of the authority of established powers, and a greater willingness on the part of ordinary people to press their own claims for rights and privileges.

In England the effects of the upheaval in the Church were particularly felt in the work of John Wycliffe (1328–84), a reformer who attacked papal authority and denounced the Great Schism as 'Antichrist itself'. He argued that every man had the right to examine the Bible for himself, and sponsored the first translation of the Bible into English. He was a major figure in the latter part of the fourteenth century, and his work led to the heretical movement known as Lollardy. It is debatable whether or not Chaucer had Lollard sympathies; certainly his writing, in particular in *The Canterbury Tales*, attacks abuses within the Church in a way with which Wycliffe would have sympathised.

Medieval beliefs

The seven deadly sins

One of the most common and enduring aspects of medieval religious **imagery** is its focus on the **seven deadly sins**, references to which are still found in modern times, long after direct belief in such a system has faded. There is occasional variation in the list of sins, but this is the most common and is listed in the order in which they appear in 'The Parson's Tale':

English	Latin
Pride	Superbia
Envy	Invidia
Anger (wrath)	Ira
Sloth	Accidia
Avarice (desire for money)	Avaricia
Gluttony (greed)	Gula
Lust (lechery)	Luxuria

Pride is traditionally the chief of the sins because it incorporates all the others. It involves a false belief in one's own importance, and is the sin through which Lucifer fell and became Satan, and through which Adam and Eve fell, tempted to believe that they could be 'as gods'.

Although occasional attempts have been made to demonstrate that the whole scheme of *The Canterbury Tales* is an exposition on the seven deadly sins, it is more fruitful to see them as an underlying part of medieval belief, and one which colours

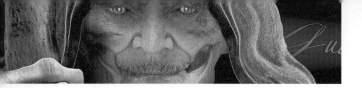

many of the portraits and the stories in *The Canterbury Tales*. Sometimes the symbolism is evident. The Wife of Bath's unrestrained sexual desire makes her guilty of lechery; the Monk is guilty of gluttony, because of his unrestrained desire for physical well-being; the Pardoner is avaricious. In other cases the particular sin of a character is more arguable; a harsh judgement of the Prioress would make her guilty of pride, whereas a more charitable one would accuse her of greed, the desire for worldly goods and status. The Merchant, who is 'Sowninge alwey th'encrees of his winning' ('The General Prologue', line 277), is a more obvious example of monetary avarice.

The four humours

Medieval science held that all matter was composed of four elements, each with its associated qualities which in turn gave rise to a human disposition known as the humour or temper. It was believed that different **humours** were predominant in individuals, dictating their temperament or 'complexioun', and that sickness arose when the balance of the humours was disturbed (an idea which survives in the modern phrase 'to be in a bad temper'). The qualities of each element, and the humour it was thought to cause, are given in the table below.

Element	Qualities	Humour	Personality
Earth	Cold and dry	Melancholy	Melancholic
Air	Hot and moist	Blood (sanguinity)	Sanguine (cheerful)
Fire	Hot and dry	Choler	Angry
Water	Cold and moist	Phlegm	Phlegmatic (unemotional)

Belief in the four humours was so ingrained in medieval society that it rarely receives specific treatment, but their consequences can be seen in a number of Chaucer's pilgrims in 'The General Prologue'. The Reeve is 'a sclendre colerik man' (line 589), his hot and dry nature having wasted his flesh away so that he is stick-like. The Franklin is also precisely identified: 'Of his complexioun he was sangwin' (line 335). The Wife of Bath has the ruddy complexion of a sanguine character too: 'Boold was hir face, and fair, and reed of hewe' (line 460). The Doctor's expertise (lines 421–23) is based on his understanding of the humours and his ability to diagnose and prescribe accordingly:

> He knew the cause of everich maladie,
> Were it of hoot, or coold, or moist, or drie,
> And where they engendred, and of what humour.

It is amusing that modern students of social behaviour often try to reduce personality to a schematic interpretation — sometimes even featuring four 'types' — that is little different from the medieval scheme.

Tradition and innovation

When reading Chaucer, it is essential to understand the different attitude to innovation that distinguishes the medieval period from the modern age. Nowadays, the emphasis in artistic creation is on originality; a writer or other artist who deliberately copies another, even with modifications, is guilty of plagiarism. School students are well aware of the dangers and the penalties incurred by including plagiarism in their essays.

In the Middle Ages, the reverse was true. Originality was viewed with extreme suspicion, while adherence to what was traditional, established and accepted was applauded. It is easier to understand this attitude by taking the medieval worldview into account. God had created the universe, the Bible was the word of God, the Earth had been created for mankind and while men and women obeyed God all was well. Everything about the world was established and fixed; the purpose of art and learning was not to discover 'new' things, but to reveal the glory and majesty of God's creation. Science, in so far as it existed at all, had the same aim.

Authorities

This attitude towards innovation helps to explain the medieval insistence on authorities — 'auctoritees' in Middle English. One could not rely on one's own opinion or judgement; instead, it was necessary to justify points by reference to accepted and established authorities. Inevitably the Bible, as the revealed word of God, was the ultimate and prime authority, closely followed by the writings of the early Church fathers, including Augustine, Jerome, Tertullian and Gregory, all of whom feature heavily in Chaucer's works. However, almost any written authority that had survived from former times was likely to be taken up and quoted as occasion served, and it is common to find classical and Arabic sources, such as Ptolemy's *Almagest*, quoted as freely as Christian ones. 'The Pardoner's Prologue and Tale' offers a clear insight into the variety and importance of authorities in medieval literature.

The writer's task was not therefore to invent new things, but to take traditional and established tales and retell them in fresh and entertaining ways. In the same way that modern folk singers are not expected to create new pieces but to offer a personal interpretation of traditional songs, so medieval artists were more highly valued when they were reusing material with which their audience would already have been familiar. Most of Chaucer's stories in *The Canterbury Tales* were well known; it is significant that where he does seem to have invented a story, as is the case in 'The Franklin's Tale', he claims that it is just a translation. The skill of the artist was in his personal interpretation and presentation of the material, and in this Chaucer excelled.

Chaucer

Chaucer's life

Although nothing is known about Chaucer as a person, and almost nothing about his private life, he was a prominent figure in the second half of the fourteenth century, with associations and positions at court. He served under three kings, and was entrusted by Edward III with foreign journeys handling the king's secret affairs. The public aspects of his life are therefore well documented, and demonstrate that he would have had direct experience of nearly all the kinds of people he represents in *The Canterbury Tales*.

There are some uncertainties and some periods of Chaucer's life for which little is known, but the salient dates are outlined below. The approximate dates for the composition of his literary works are also given.

Key dates and works

c. 1340–45	Geoffrey Chaucer born, son of a London wine merchant.
1357	Becomes a page in the household of the Countess of Ulster.
1360	Captured while serving in France; ransomed by Edward III.
1366	Journeys to Spain; marries Philippa Rouet around this time.
1367	Appointed Yeoman of the Chamber in the king's household.
1367–77	Journeys abroad on the king's business.
1369	Campaigns in France; appointed Esquire in the king's household.
Pre-1372	*The Book of the Duchess*.
1372–73	First journey to Italy.
1372–80	*The House of Fame*.
1374	Appointed Comptroller of Customs and Subsidy.
1377	Edward III dies; accession of Richard II.
1378	Second journey to Italy.
1380–86	*The Parliament of Fowls; Troilus and Criseyde; The Legend of Good Women*.
1385	Appointed Justice of the Peace for Kent.
1385–1400	*The Canterbury Tales*.
1386	Sits in Parliament as Knight of the Shire for Kent.
1389	Appointed Clerk to the King's Works.
1391	Appointed Subforester.
1394	Awarded extra grant for good service.
1399	Richard II deposed; accession of Henry IV.
	Previous grants confirmed by Henry IV.
1400	Dies on 25 October; buried in Westminster Abbey.

Chaucer and his contemporaries

Chaucer's place in the history of English literature

It was John Dryden in the seventeenth century who labelled Chaucer 'the father of English poetry'. The modern reader may share this belief, because Chaucer is the earliest writer who is still widely known. His language is the most accessible, and the most 'modern', of all the medieval authors, and his emphasis on apparently realistic characters and themes seems modern too. He championed the use of the **iambic pentameter** and the rhyming **couplet** in much of his work, and this **metre** became the staple of English verse for the next 500 years. He was well known both in his own lifetime and after; many writers, including Shakespeare, were influenced by him and used his work as a source. The term 'father of English poetry' thus contains considerable truth, but it is also a distortion and conceals facts of which the student of Chaucer needs to be aware.

Chaucer died 600 years ago in 1400. *Beowulf*, the earliest known masterpiece in English, was composed around AD 700. By that reckoning, Chaucer lived more than half way through the chronological history of English literature and represents part of a continuing tradition rather than being the inventor of a new one.

It is easy to explain both the error contained in the popular view of Chaucer and his pre-eminence. First, there is the matter of language. *Beowulf* was composed in Anglo-Saxon (also known as Old English), and even Chaucer's great contemporaries, such as William Langland and the anonymous author of *Sir Gawain and the Green Knight*, were writing in a style that dated back nearly 1,000 years. This was the so-called 'alliterative style', in which **alliteration** and a flexible **rhythm** were used to give lines shape and structure. In contrast, Chaucer wrote in a newfangled style influenced by French and Italian, using a set metre (mainly iambic pentameter in *The Canterbury Tales*) and rhyming couplets. His language was that used in London, and since London was the capital of England it was inevitable that Chaucer's language would be that which has come to predominate, and is therefore most familiar to subsequent generations. Moreover, until Chaucer's day there was very little 'literature' at all, in the sense of material that was ever written down. In a largely illiterate society, most culture was communicated orally, and written versions (including *Beowulf* itself) are fortuitous historical accidents. Most writing was done in Latin, the language of the educated (which essentially meant monks), and it is only from Chaucer's time onwards that there is a strong tradition of literature written in English.

Other works

Chaucer did not just write *The Canterbury Tales*. His other major work is *Troilus and Criseyde*, an 8,200-line poem written in a **metre** known as **rhyme** royal, a

7-line stanza in iambic pentameter, which he used in 'The Clerk's Tale' and 'The Prioress's Tale'. It is a tragic love story based on a supposed incident in the Trojan War; Chaucer borrowed the plot from Boccaccio, and it was later treated by Shakespeare and Dryden.

Chaucer also wrote a number of short verses, and several long poems of the type known as 'dream visions', in which the narrator falls asleep and dreams the events the poem relates. His interest in the status and role of women, a noticeable theme in *The Canterbury Tales*, is confirmed by *The Legend of Good Women*, which tells the stories of nine classical heroines, including Cleopatra and Thisbe.

Chaucer is famed for his wide reading and considerable education, which are illustrated by the fact that a number of his works are translations. He may have translated part of *La Roman de la Rose*, the vast thirteenth-century French poem that is a major source for and influence on Chaucer's own work. He translated from Latin *The Consolation of Philosophy* by Boethius, one of the best-known philosophical works in the Middle Ages (although it dates from the sixth century). Finally, he translated a scientific work, *A Treatise on the Astrolabe* (an instrument for measuring the position of the stars), which demonstrates the breadth of Chaucer's knowledge as well as confirming the interest in astrology visible throughout his work, for example in the description of the Doctor of Physic in 'The General Prologue', and the detail of Nicholas's learning in 'The Miller's Tale'.

Influences

A man as widely read as Chaucer would be familiar with all the great historical writers known in his time, together with many contemporaries. In addition, Chaucer's foreign travels on the king's business would have brought him into direct contact with the works of great European writers such as Boccaccio and Petrarch. Boccaccio's *Decameron* became a direct model for *The Canterbury Tales*. Chaucer was heavily influenced by biblical and religious writings, and by French and Italian writers of his own and previous centuries. It is worth thinking of him as a European rather than as a primarily English writer.

Numerous influences and sources, both general and specific, have been identified, and you should consult the edition of your text to appreciate the wealth of material on which Chaucer draws.

Contemporaries

Chaucer is the best known of the fourteenth-century writers, but during this period there was a huge flowering of writing in English. This was probably because English was re-emerging as the official language of the country after three centuries of Norman French domination, and because greater education and literacy allowed the production of true literature, i.e work that was composed in writing rather than orally.

In Chaucer's own lifetime there were two other major English writers whose importance rivals that of Chaucer — William Langland and the Gawain-poet.

Langland

William Langland wrote the great poem *Piers Plowman*. He was obsessed with the work and wrote three versions of it, ranging from 2,500 to 7,300 lines, over a period of 30 or 40 years. It is written in the alliterative style, a completely different form of poetry from Chaucer's, and one which was a development of Anglo-Saxon verse. *Piers Plowman* is a vast allegorical work in which Piers begins as the figure of a humble ploughman (comparable to the Ploughman of 'The General Prologue') and ends up as an allegorical representation of Christ. It is deeply serious, complex, and unique.

The Gawain-poet

Meanwhile, perhaps in Cheshire, there was a poet to whom authorship of all four of the poems preserved in the *Pearl* manuscript is usually attributed. The poet's name is not known, but he is most commonly referred to as the Gawain-poet, after his most famous work, *Sir Gawain and the Green Knight*. Like *Piers Plowman*, this poem is written in an alliterative verse form, but its language is now so unfamiliar that it is usually read in a modernised version. It tells the story of a mysterious Green Knight who challenges King Arthur's court to a 'game' at Christmas. He invites someone to chop his head off, but when Gawain does so the Green Knight calmly collects his head and demands the right to return the blow in a year's time. The rest of the poem follows Gawain's dilemmas and tests as he seeks to keep his side of the bargain. The poem is a powerful, complex work that manages to be simultaneously humane and witty, profoundly moral and symbolic.

As well as these two writers there was John Gower, a personal friend of Chaucer's and a major influence on him, but whose works are no longer held in such esteem. He is best known for his *Confessio Amantis*.

The existence of these writers points to a vernacular tradition of enormous richness, variety and substance of which only a small portion has survived into the modern age. As well as Langland, the Gawain-poet and Gower, there was a wealth of material in all forms (poetry, drama and religious prose) that shows how Chaucer was part of a great age of literary output, rather than an isolated and unique genius.

Story collections

In the Middle Ages, storytelling was a common form of communal entertainment. Literacy was scarce, and tales were told and retold, handed down from storyteller to storyteller through generations and centuries. Originally, almost all stories would have been in verse as this made them easier to remember, but as the Middle Ages progressed an increasing number were written in prose. Traditional stories might be gathered together by a scribe, and gradually individual storytellers emerged who adapted material to their own designs and added to it. Collections of stories therefore became common, some of which were mere agglomerations of tales, and others unified and written by a single author. A few of these collections are still well known, the most familiar example being *The Thousand and One Nights*.

Influences and contemporary examples

Chaucer would have been influenced by two particular works. The anonymous *Gesta Romanorum* was an amorphous and disparate group of tales gathered in various forms over a long period, but united by a single guiding principle. The tales, many of them traditional or legendary, were viewed as allegories, that is to say literal **narratives** that could be given a parallel spiritual interpretation. Each tale is followed by an explanation offering a Christian reading of the text. For example, the classical tale of Atalanta, the swift runner who is beaten by a competitor who throws golden apples to distract her from the race, is seen as an **allegory** of the human soul being tempted by the devil. It is worth considering how far *The Canterbury Tales* can similarly be seen as a diverse group of stories unified by an underlying Christian message. The *Gesta Romanorum* is also a vital reminder that medieval literature could be complex, and that medieval audiences expected multiple and concealed meanings in a work of art.

The second work, which may be considered as an immediate model for Chaucer, is the *Decameron* by Giovanni Boccaccio. Chaucer travelled to Italy and may have met Boccaccio; it is certainly true that he knew the Italian poet's work and was probably trying to create an equivalent masterpiece in English. The framework of the *Decameron* is similar to that of *The Canterbury Tales*, in that 10 narrators are given the task of telling 10 stories each over the course of 10 days, making a neat 100 stories in all. Chaucer's scheme has 30 narrators telling four stories each, making a more substantial total of 120 tales. The fact that this scheme came nowhere near completion, and that Chaucer probably reduced the plan to a single tale for each teller, does not reduce the significance of the comparison.

Chaucer's friend John Gower also produced a story collection, suggesting the popularity of such works in the fourteenth century. Gower's *Confessio Amantis* (*Confession of the Lover*) is a moral work commenting on the seven deadly sins, the same theme as the sermon in 'The Parson's Tale'. Gower also used some of the same stories as Chaucer, notably the tale of Florent (also told by the Wife of Bath) and the tale of Constance ('The Man of Law's Tale').

The Canterbury Tales as a story collection

The difference between Chaucer's work and these other story collections is the dynamic link between the tellers and the tales. The *Gesta Romanorum* has no narrator at all; it is merely a collection of separate tales. Although there are ten separate narrators in the *Decameron*, there is no great significance in who tells which tale. In Chaucer's work, the match of tale and teller is frequently a crucial part of the overall meaning. The Knight, the most courtly figure on the pilgrimage, tells a suitably courtly tale. The Miller, the most vulgar of the pilgrims, tells the coarsest story. In the most sophisticated case, the Pardoner, who would be a profitable subject for modern psychoanalysis, introduces his tale by explaining the hypocritical success of his own sales techniques, and then proceeds to attempt to dupe his auditors in exactly the same way. As part of this he tells a devastatingly effective tale of avaricce and justice, which is integrally linked to both his personality and his practices.

The Canterbury Tales is remarkable because it contains examples of all the kinds of story popular in the medieval period — courtly tales, sermons, saints' lives, **fabliaux**, animal fables — and different verse forms, as well as two tales in prose. This makes *The Canterbury Tales* one of the most diverse of all story collections, and the **narrative** device of the pilgrimage plays an important part in giving this mix cohesion.

It can be difficult to appreciate the significance of Chaucer's overall scheme, both because of the unfinished nature of *The Canterbury Tales*, and because A-level students are usually restricted to studying a tale in isolation. It is strongly recommended that you acquaint yourself with *The Canterbury Tales* as a whole, perhaps by reading the complete work in Modern English.

Chaucer's audience and purpose

Audience

Chaucer was a courtly writer, composing his works for a courtly and sophisticated audience. In earlier eras, almost all culture would have been oral and communal, with storytellers and poets reciting their works to diverse groups of listeners. The only 'books' were manuscripts that were copied by hand onto parchment made from animal skins, and would have been rare and valuable. Almost all manuscripts were of religious texts, and it was not until the later Middle Ages that manuscripts of secular works like Chaucer's became available (more than 80 copies of *The Canterbury Tales* survive). By Chaucer's time, there were sufficient numbers of educated people and manuscript copies to enable private reading parties where one person, for example a lady of the court, would read stories to small groups of friends. An individual might even read stories alone, but that would necessitate the availability of a manuscript, and leisure to peruse it.

Despite these developments, the main mode of communication was still the public performance. It is helpful to think of Chaucer's original audience listening to *The Canterbury Tales* rather than reading them. No doubt Chaucer read his work to groups at court on frequent occasions, and his audience was mixed, with members of different social groups and classes present. In this sense, Chaucer's situation would have been similar to that of Shakespeare, who had to construct dramas that would appeal to the widest possible taste and intellect. *The Canterbury Tales* includes plenty of entertaining moments to elicit the most superficial of responses, yet also contains subtle and sophisticated elements.

Another development was that Chaucer was identified by name as an author and was popular in his own lifetime. Before this, almost all art was anonymous — the work of art mattered, not its creator.

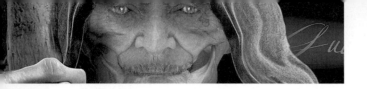

Purpose

This consideration of Chaucer's audience leads to the vexed question of Chaucer's intentions in composing *The Canterbury Tales*, a subject to which there is no definitive answer.

Irony

Irony is the dominant **tone** throughout *The Canterbury Tales*, and this makes Chaucer's work elusive and his purpose difficult to define. Irony always depends on personal interpretation, but not all interpretations are equally justifiable or defensible, so be sure that yours are based on wide and careful reading.

An example will illustrate the need for thought. Consider lines 630–32 of 'The Pardoner's Tale':

> And Jhesu Crist, that is oure soules leche,
> So grunte yow his paroun to receive,
> For that is best; I wol yow nat deceive.

An inattentive reader might note this as a conventional preacher's comment, and pass on. A more considered response is to examine the immediate context. The Pardoner has just completed his tale of the rioters and explained that it is an example of the stories he uses in his sermons. It seems that he is genuinely telling the pilgrims that Christ's pardon is what is truly needed. But this is the Pardoner, who is trying to sell his own indulgences. His claim that he will not deceive them is precisely false: deceiving them is exactly what he intends to do. He is trying to lull the pilgrims with a falsehood, so that he can then begin the 'hard sell' of offering them his own wares. Furthermore, the reader will recall that the Pardoner is the person most in need of Christ's mercy. Finally, it will be noted that the Pardoner's hypocrisy does not invalidate what he says; Christ's pardon truly is the best thing to which a sinner can aspire. All these aspects need to be considered, and a good A-level student will be able to handle the sophisticated response required.

Possible interpretations

Modern readers must make up their own minds as to what they are going to gain from studying Chaucer, and this is often a reflection of what they bring to their studies. You will probably find evidence for all the approaches suggested below, but it is up to you to decide what Chaucer has to offer, and how he is to be interpreted in the twenty-first century.

Entertainment

Chaucer's tales are entertaining, and some readers wish to look no further than that. John Carrington, in *Our Greatest Writers and their Major Works* (How To Books, 2003), says simply: 'Chaucer has no over-arching moral or philosophical intention', and that he 'is driven by a curiosity and sympathy for life that excludes the judgemental'.

Social comment

Many readers find some degree of comment on the behaviour and manners of medieval society. This could be anything from wry observation to serious **satire**, e.g. a satire on the three estates class system or a developed thesis on the nature of marriage.

Moral teaching

Chaucer himself, in the 'Retraction' included at the end of *The Canterbury Tales*, quotes from St Paul's comment in the New Testament that all literature contains a moral lesson.

Devotional literature

As a development of the previous point, readers may consider the Christian framework of *The Canterbury Tales* and the idea that it preaches specifically Christian doctrines. The vast majority of medieval literature is religious in this sense, e.g. the mystery plays, such as the Coventry and York cycles, are based on Bible stories. *The Canterbury Tales* finishes with 'The Parson's Tale', a sermon about the seven deadly sins, encouraging many to interpret them as having a Christian message about behaviour and morality.

Allegory

Medieval people were familiar with allegory, in which a surface narrative contains one or more further parallel layers of meaning. Such ideas were familiar from Christ's parables in the Bible, and the whole Bible was interpreted allegorically in the Middle Ages. It is possible to see Chaucer as an allegorist in whole or part; Robert P. Miller, writing in the *Companion to Chaucer Studies* (Oxford University Press, 1968), comments: 'Each pilgrim tells his tale from his own point of view, but this point of view is finally to be measured in the perspective afforded by the allegorical system.'

The Canterbury Tales

The framework of *The Canterbury Tales*

'The General Prologue' introduces *The Canterbury Tales* and establishes the framework that will underpin the diverse collection of tales that follow. It is worth considering the *Tales* as a whole to see what Chaucer was trying to achieve. It is well known that Chaucer left the work unfinished when he died in 1400, and it has traditionally been assumed that we have only a fragmentary part of what he would eventually have written.

The tales and their tellers

Chaucer's original plan, as revealed in 'The General Prologue', allowed for 30 pilgrims telling four tales each, making a total of 120 tales in all. However, only 24 tales exist, four of which are unfinished, and although as the *Tales* stand nearly every pilgrim tells a tale, they only tell one each.

It is clear that Chaucer drastically modified his original plan, although he never altered 'The General Prologue' to confirm this. There is an excellent reason for his changes. In Chaucer's hands, the tales and tellers are matched with great care, so that one illuminates the other. This is conspicuously true of characters such as the Wife of Bath and the Pardoner. To give these characters more than one tale would gain nothing, and would in fact weaken the effectiveness of the link between tale and teller. In this way Chaucer breaks out of the traditional mould of story collections, in which the character of the narrator is largely unimportant; *The Thousand and One Nights*, for example, has a single narrator for all of its diverse stories.

The significance of the connection between the pilgrims and their tales is emphasised by the only character to tell two tales: Chaucer himself. He starts off with the tale of 'Sir Thopas', but this is told so feebly that the Host (hardly the most astute of critics) interrupts him and tells him to stop. Chaucer thereby achieves the double effect of satirising the weak and formulaic narrative verse of his own time, and creating a joke against himself. His revenge is to let the pilgrim Chaucer follow up with 'a lytel thing in prose', the extended and deeply moral 'Tale of Melibee'. Given that the only other prose piece in *The Canterbury Tales* is 'The Parson's Tale', a meditation on penance, the author may well intend that the pilgrim Chaucer's tale be regarded as one of the most important pieces in the collection, although it is not at all to modern taste.

It is therefore likely that *The Canterbury Tales* is much nearer to completion than a consideration of Chaucer's original plan suggests. However, there are certain anomalies that Chaucer would have needed to address:

- The Yeoman, the Ploughman and the Five Guildsmen lack tales. The absence of 'The Ploughman's Tale' is a particular loss, given the iconic status of ploughmen, as established by Chaucer's contemporary William Langland in *Piers Plowman*.
- 'The Cook's Tale' and 'The Squire's Tale' are unfinished and simply break off part way through; the Knight interrupts the Monk, and the Host halts the doggerel tale of 'Sir Thopas'.
- There are occasional discrepancies in the assignation of tales to tellers; e.g. 'The Shipman's Tale' is clearly intended to have a female narrator.
- In several cases there is no significant connection between tale and teller, although this may be intentional.
- Some of the tales do not have links between them, and the final sequence of the tales is not established.

Taken as a whole, however, it is possible to discern a powerful and unified work that closely reflects Chaucer's final intentions.

The table below shows the order in which the pilgrims are introduced in 'The General Prologue' and the length of their tales.

Character	Lines in 'The General Prologue'	Number of lines	Tale	Number of lines in tale	Order in The Riverside Chaucer
1 Knight	43–78	36	'The Knight's Tale'	2,250	1
2 Squire	79–100	22	'The Squire's Tale'	664	11 (unfinished)
3 Yeoman	101–17	17	–	–	–
4 Prioress	118–62	45	'The Prioress's Tale'	203	16
5 Second Nun	163–64	$1\frac{1}{2}$	'The Second Nun's Tale'	434	21
6–8 Three Priests	164	$\frac{1}{2}$	'The Nun's Priest's Tale'	626	20
9 Monk	165–207	43	'The Monk's Tale'	776	19 (unfinished)
10 Friar	208–69	62	'The Friar's Tale'	364	7
11 Merchant	270–84	15	'The Merchant's Tale'	1,174	10
12 Clerk	285–308	24	'The Clerk's Tale'	1,120	9
13 Man of Law	309–30	22	'The Man of Law's Tale'	1,028	5
14 Franklin	331–60	30	'The Franklin's Tale'	896	12
15–19 Five Guildsmen	361–78	18	–	–	–
20 Cook	379–87	9	'The Cook's Tale'	58	4 (unfinished)
21 Shipman	388–410	23	'The Shipman's Tale'	434	15
22 Doctor of Physic	411–44	34	'The Physician's Tale'	286	13
23 Wife of Bath	445–76	32	'The Wife of Bath's Tale'	408	6
24 Parson	477–528	52	'The Parson's Tale'	1.005 (prose)	24
25 Ploughman	529–41	13	–	–	–
26 Miller	542–66	25	'The Miller's Tale'	668	2
27 Manciple	567–86	20	'The Manciple's Tale'	258	23
28 Reeve	587–622	36	'The Reeve's Tale'	403	3
29 Summoner	623–68	46	'The Summoner's Tale'	586	8
30 Pardoner	669–714	46	'The Pardoner's Tale'	506	14
31 Chaucer	–	–	'Sir Thopas'	207	17 (unfinished)
			'The Tale of Melibee'	922 (prose)	18
32 Canon	–	–	–	–	–
33 Canon's Yeoman	–	–	'The Canon's Yeoman's Tale'	762	22

Pilgrimage

The Canterbury Tales is based on two great defining structures: the story collection and the pilgrimage. The latter serves two purposes in the work. First, it is a **narrative** device, and second, it has a **thematic** function.

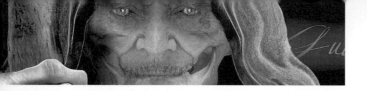

Narrative device

The role of pilgrimage in framing the narrative is simple but important. It gives Chaucer a basic plot — 30 pilgrims travel from London to Canterbury and back again — within which he can set out the multiple and varied narratives of his characters. It allows him to gather together a complete cross-section of the social hierarchy (excluding royalty, who would have travelled separately, and the very lowest serfs, who would not have been able to leave their work), in circumstances in which the characters can mingle on terms of near equality. This equality would have existed as regards their journey and experiences, but crucially there is equality of opportunity; every pilgrim gets the chance to tell a story, and every story receives the same attention, although what the pilgrims choose to do with their opportunities is another matter. The pilgrimage is also dynamic, so that circumstances on the journey can impinge on the storytelling framework, as happens when the pilgrims encounter a canon whose yeoman tells a tale of his own.

Thematic function

The second function of the pilgrimage in *The Canterbury Tales* is even more important. A pilgrimage has two aspects: it is a journey, but it is also a sacred journey. Both elements are crucial to an understanding of Chaucer's work.

Journeys

The image of the journey has always been central to human understanding. Life itself is conventionally seen as a journey from birth to death, and so any physical journey can be viewed as an image of life, with the travellers gaining experience as they progress. A pilgrimage is a special kind of physical journey, where the goal is a holy or sacred place. The parallel with the journey of life gains an extra significance, because the pilgrimage's sacred purpose is the equivalent of the soul's journey through life towards God. The best-known form of pilgrimage in modern times is the Muslim pilgrimage to Mecca, a journey that every devout Muslim is supposed to undertake at least once.

Holy sites and shrines

In the Middle Ages the pilgrimage was a common and popular activity and there were innumerable holy places to visit. The most holy site of all was Jerusalem, which the Wife of Bath visited three times, and Chaucer also mentions some of the other most famous ones, particularly Santiago de Compostela in Spain. In England, the shrine of Thomas Becket in Canterbury was the most popular destination following Becket's assassination in 1170, and it would remain so until it was destroyed by Henry VIII in the 1530s.

The importance of shrines lay in people's belief in the efficacy of saints and holy relics, as is evident from Chaucer's portrayal of the Pardoner. The Catholic Church taught that God could not be approached directly; it was therefore necessary to pray to those closest to him to intercede. Along with the Virgin Mary, with her unique position as the mother of Christ, the saints were thought to be endowed with special powers and influence. The relics of saints, particularly their bones, were held to have mystical, almost magical powers, and there were dozens of shrines associated with particular saints, each usually venerated for a specific quality.

Travel

Pilgrimage therefore held an important place in medieval life, but it was also a way to travel. In an insecure world, there was safety in numbers as well as the pleasure of company. Some of Chaucer's pilgrims, such as the Guildsmen, would be delighted to have a knight as part of the group, because he could offer practical as well as symbolic protection. A woman like the Wife of Bath would be pleased that the Guildsmen themselves were there, among whom she might look for her sixth husband; it would also have been difficult for her as a woman to travel alone.

It has been said that medieval pilgrimages were the equivalent of modern package holidays, and there is some value in the **analogy**, at least if it is seen as indicating the impulse to travel and the willingness of diverse people to band together for convenience and economies of scale. The comparison falls down, however, when the purpose of travel is considered. Modern holidaymakers largely seek pleasure, and few travel with an overtly spiritual purpose. The reverse was true in the Middle Ages; although a few of Chaucer's pilgrims might have purely social or secular motives for the journey, most would have a greater or lesser degree of devotion, and all would have been aware of the sacred significance of their journey, even if they sometimes chose to ignore it.

Symbolism

Every character, every tale, and every word of *The Canterbury Tales* is contained within the symbolic framework of the pilgrimage, whether the individual characters are aware of it or not. When the Parson tells his tale of sin and repentance the connection is obvious, but the symbolism of the pilgrimage is equally relevant when the Merchant is telling his tale of an ill-judged marriage, when the Miller and the Reeve are trading tales at each other's expense, or when the Pardoner tries to con his audience through the techniques that he has just exposed. Every one of these is measured against, and judged by, the sacred context in which their journey and their lives take place.

The route to Canterbury

The map (overleaf) shows the details of the pilgrimage in *The Canterbury Tales*, including the places mentioned by Chaucer in the text. The journey from London to Canterbury was nearly 60 miles long and would usually have taken several days in each direction.

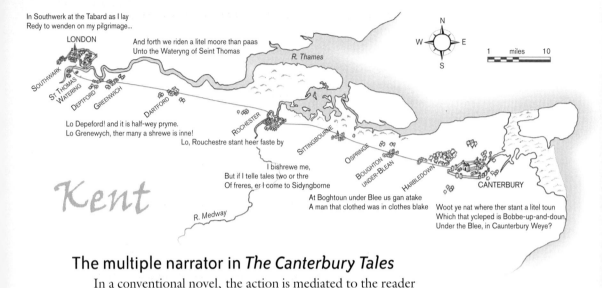

In Southwerk at the Tabard as I lay
Redy to wenden on my pilgrimage...

LONDON

And forth we riden a litel moore than paas
Unto the Wateryng of Seint Thomas

R. Thames

N
W — E
S

1   miles   10

SOUTHWARK
ST THOMAS WATERING
DEPTFORD
GREENWICH
DARTFORD

Lo Depeford! and it is half-wey pryme.
Lo Grenewych, ther many a shrewe is inne!

ROCHESTER

Lo, Rouchestre stant heer faste by

SITTINGBOURNE

I bishrewe me,
But if I telle tales two or thre
Of freres, er I come to Sidyngborne

OSPRINGE
BOUGHTON UNDER-BLEAN
HARBLEDOWN

CANTERBURY

At Boghtoun under Blee us gan atake
A man that clothed was in clothes blake

Woot ye nat where ther stant a litel toun
Which that ycleped is Bobbe-up-and-doun,
Under the Blee, in Caunterbury Weye?

Kent

R. Medway

The multiple narrator in *The Canterbury Tales*

In a conventional novel, the action is mediated to the reader
by a narrator:

Narrator
⬇
Audience

In *The Canterbury Tales*, Chaucer introduces further narrative levels that offer the
opportunity for much greater subtlety. First, Chaucer the author introduces himself
as a character or persona within the text, so that the situation is as follows:

Chaucer the author
⬇
Chaucer the pilgrim
⬇
Audience

This means that when you come across a remark in 'The General Prologue' like 'And
I seyde his opinion was good', it is ostensibly made by Chaucer the pilgrim. The
reader must decide how far it may also be Chaucer the author's view.

When it comes to the tales themselves, a further layer of complexity is added
because each tale is told by one of the pilgrims, and reported by Chaucer the
pilgrim. The narrative therefore reaches its audience at three removes from its
author:

Chaucer the author
⬇
Chaucer the pilgrim
⬇
Pilgrim narrator
⬇
Audience

Finally, when a character within one of the tales speaks a fifth narrative layer is added:

Chaucer the author

Chaucer the pilgrim

Pilgrim narrator

Character

Audience

The attentive reader must decide how far each of the narrating figures is in accord with what is being said. For example, the rioter in 'The Pardoner's Tale' asks rhetorically of Death:

> Is it swich peril with him for to meete? (line 407)

The reader needs to consider whether the rioter can so completely underestimate Death (he can, under the influence of drink), how far the Pardoner seems to share this arrogance (he knows he is a sinner, but shows no signs of repenting and thus faces eternal death), what Chaucer the pilgrim's view would be (probable amusement at the rioter's naivety), and finally what Chaucer the author intends to convey about the nature of behaviour and pride in the context of the whole of 'The Pardoner's Prologue and Tale'. This last question is simultaneously the most important and, because of all the intervening narrative layers, the most concealed, and it is why critical debate about Chaucer is unending. In this case he presumably wants the audience to consider the rhetorical question both as it applies to the rioter in the story, and how it applies to the Pardoner in the context of *The Canterbury Tales*. A sophisticated reading is required. This is easier for the modern reader who has time to dwell over the text, where Chaucer's original audience would frequently only hear the tales read to them.

Chaucer the pilgrim as narrator

The subtlety in Chaucer's craft arises from the device of the pilgrim narrator. This persona is portrayed as a sociable but rather diffident character. When the time comes for him to tell his own tale the Host thinks he looks 'elvyssh' (otherworldly) and shy: 'For evere upon the ground I se thee stare' ('Prologue to Sir Thopas', line 697). Chaucer the pilgrim begins to tell a very poor story ('Sir Thopas'), but once interrupted by the Host he launches into a long, moral, prose narrative ('The Tale of Melibee'), which shows his erudition and seriousness. In 'The General Prologue', Chaucer the pilgrim frequently appears to be naive, most famously when he agrees with the Monk's low opinion of his own vows ('And I seyde his opinion was good', line 183). Often this encourages the other pilgrims to make further indiscreet confessions about their behaviour, such as the Monk revealing his obsession

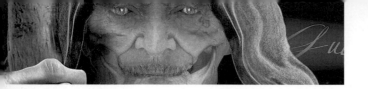

with hunting and riding. When he does wish to comment directly on a character, he can do so, as in the case of the Summoner: 'But wel I woot he lied right in dede' (line 661).

Chaucer's verse

The metre that Chaucer adopted for most of *The Canterbury Tales* became the standard one used in English poetry for the next 500 years, and in this sense at least he should be familiar to the modern reader. He writes in iambic pentameter, the metre used by Shakespeare, Milton, Keats and all of the great poets prior to the twentieth century. The lines are arranged into pairs called **heroic couplets**, a grand style often undermined by its content.

'Iambic' refers to the rhythm of the verse: a repeated pattern of two syllables, with the first syllable being unstressed and the second syllable being stressed, as in words like 'remind' and 'believe'. An iamb is one of these two-syllable, unstressed/stressed patterns. Each pair of syllables is called a foot. 'Pentameter' (literally five measures or 'feet') means that five feet are joined together to make a ten-syllable (decasyllabic) regular line: da dum da dum da dum da dum da dum. The conventional mark for a stressed syllable is /, and the mark for an unstressed syllable is ~. A couplet of iambic pentameter therefore goes like this:

> ~ / ~ / ~ / ~ / ~ /
> Bifil that in that seson on a day,
> ~ / ~ / ~ / ~ / ~/
> In Southwerk at the Tabard as I lay   ('The General Prologue', lines 19–20)

The reason that this became the staple metre of English poetry is because iambic rhythm is closest to natural speech — whenever you speak a sentence, it contains more iambs than any other rhythm. Chaucer shows astonishing assurance and versatility in handling the iambic form. He can use it for formal description in a stately manner:

> In Flaundres whilom was a compaignye
> Of yonge folk that haunteden folye,
> As riot, hasard, stywes, and tavernes.   ('The Pardoner's Tale', lines 177–79)

He can use it for fast-paced action:

> And with that word it happed him, par cas,
> To take the botel ther the poison was,
> And drank, and yaf his felawe drinke also,
> For which anon they storven bothe two.   (ibid., lines 599–602)

He uses it for rhetorical effect:

> O cursed sinne of alle cursednesse!
> O traitours homicide, O wikkednesse!
> O glotonye, luxurie, and hasardrye!   (ibid., lines 609–11)

But most frequently and most effectively he uses it to represent speech:

> Lo, how deere, shortly for to sayn,
> Aboght was thilke cursed vileynye. (ibid., lines 216–17)

> 'Nay, nay,' quod he, 'thanne have I Cristes curs!
> Lat be,' quod he, 'it shal nat be, so theech!' (ibid., lines 660–61)

In his earlier work, Chaucer frequently used an octosyllabic (eight-syllable) line, which was common at the time; the iambic pentameter marks his maturity as a poet.

Chaucer's language

There is no doubt that the Middle English of *The Canterbury Tales* comes between the modern reader and an easy appreciation of the work. However, after a little practice most of the difficulties presented by the language drop away. Note that the vocabulary can present problems, because some words look familiar or obvious, and aren't. For example, the word 'wood' can mean wood but, in a different context, means mad, as in the description of the Host in the Introduction to 'The Pardoner's Tale' (line 1). The solution is to keep a careful eye on the notes and glossary of your edition.

Reading aloud

The easiest way to start to understand Chaucer's language is to read it aloud, or to listen to it being read. Chaucer intended his verse to be spoken, and it makes more sense when it is. Remember the following:

- Most letters are pronounced, so that 'knight' sounds like 'cnicht' and 'mighte' like 'micht'.
- The final 'e' on words like 'fooles' ('fool-es') is normally pronounced, unless it is followed by another vowel.
- Some vowels have different sound values, but don't worry about this initially.
- Words imported from French would still sound French, so 'dotage' would be 'dotarge' and 'mariage' would be 'mar-ee-arge'.

With these few simple adjustments, aim to read the verse as if it were ordinary conversation. Try to ignore the rhythm and rhyme — they'll take care of themselves. Your edition should have further detail on aspects of pronunciation, but the primary objective is to get a sense of the flow of the language.

Modernisations

Another good way of gaining confidence in reading the language is to create a Modern English version of each line. This can be done aloud in class, or you can jot down a literal version as you go along, for example:

> In Flaundres whilom was a compaigne
> *In Flanders once upon a time there was a group*

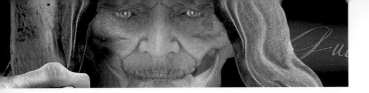

Of yonge folk that haunteden folye
Of young people who behaved foolishly

It isn't long before Chaucer's English becomes almost as straightforward as Shakespeare's. You never quite lose your caution in looking at it (as you shouldn't with Shakespeare), but you do become more comfortable working with it.

It may be a good idea to obtain a modern version of 'The Pardoner's Prologue and Tale', and even of the whole of *The Canterbury Tales*. This will allow you to check your own rendering of each line, so that you are confident that you have the correct basic meaning.

The Pardoner in 'The General Prologue'

This is how the Pardoner is introduced in 'The General Prologue' (lines 671–716). The modernised English version (in italics) is entirely literal, and is given to help clarify the meaning of the passage.

With him* ther rood a gentil Pardoner	*the Summoner
With him there rode a worthy Pardoner	
Of Rouncivale, his freend and his compeer*,	*close friend
From Rouncivale, his friend and ally,	
That streight was comen fro the court of Rome.	
Who had come straight from the papal court in Rome.	
Ful loude he soong 'Com hider, love, to me!'	
Loudly he sang: 'Come hither, love, to me!'	
This Somonour bar to him a stif burdoun*;	*bass
The Summoner accompanied him;	
Was nevere trompe* of half so greet a soun.	*trumpet
No trumpet was ever half as loud.	
This Pardoner hadde heer as yelow as wex,	
This Pardoner had hair as yellow as wax,	
But smothe it heeng as dooth a strike of flex*;	*flax
But it hung down smoothly like flax;	
By ounces* henge his lokkes that he hadde,	*small bunches
What he had hung in loose bunches,	
And therwith he his shuldres overspradde;	
And he spread these over his shoulders;	

But thinne it lay, by colpons* oon and oon.   *strips
But it lay thinly in separate clusters.

But hood, for jolitee, wered he noon,
To appear jolly he didn't wear a hood,

For it was trussed up in his walet*.   *bag
Which was trussed up in his bag.

Hym thoughte he rood al of the newe jet*;   *fashion
He thought he rode in the latest fashion;

Dischevelee*, save his cappe*, he rood al bare.   *dishevelled   * skull-cap
He rode dishevelled and bare-headed apart from his skull-cap.

Swiche glarynge eyen* hadde he as an hare.   *eyes
He had bulging eyes like a hare.

A vernicle* hadde he sowed upon his cappe.   *an image of Saint Veronica
He had a Veronica sewn on his cap.

His walet lay biforn him in his lappe,
His bag lay before him in his lap,

Bretful* of pardoun, comen from Rome al hoot.   *brimful
Brimful of pardons hot from Rome.

A voys he hadde as smal* as hath a goot.   *high
He had a high voice like a goat.

No berd hadde he, ne nevere sholde have;
He had no beard, and never would have —

As smothe it was as it were late shave.
His skin was smooth as if newly shaved.

I trowe he were a gelding* or a mare.   *castrated horse
I think he was a eunuch or a mare.

But of his craft, fro Berwik into Ware,
But as to his craft, from Berwick to Ware

Ne was ther swich another pardoner.
There wasn't a pardoner to match him.

For in his male* he hadde a pilwe-beer*,   *bag   *pillow-case
In his bag he had a pillow-case

Which that he seyde was Oure Lady veil:
Which he said was Our Lady's veil;

He seyde he hadde a gobet of the seil
He said he had a piece of the sail

That Seint Peter hadde, whan that he wente
That Saint Peter used, when he went

Upon the see, til Jhesu Crist hym hente*.   *took
To sea, before Jesus called him.

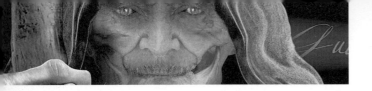

He hadde a crois of latoun* ful of stones,   *brass
He had a brass cross set with stones,

And in a glas* he hadde pigges bones.   *case
And in a case he had pigs' bones.

But with thise relikes, whan that he fond
But with these relics, when he found

A povre person* dwellinge upon lond,   *priest
A poor priest living in some place,

Upon a day he gat him moore moneye
In one day he made more money

Than that the person gat in monthes tweye;
Than the priest earned in two months.

And thus, with feyned flaterie and japes*,   *tricks
And so, with false flattery and tricks,

He made the person and the peple his apes.
He made monkeys of the priest and people.

But trewely to tellen atte laste,
But to tell truly at the end,

He was in chirche a noble ecclesiaste*.   *cleric
In church he was a noble cleric.

Wel koude he rede a lessoun or a storie,
He knew well how to read a lesson or sermon,

But alderbest* he song an offertorie*;   *best of all *offertory hymn
But best of all he sung the Offertory,

For wel he wiste, whan that song was songe,
For he knew very well that when that song was sung

He moste preche and wel affile* his tonge   *smooth
He must preach and smooth his tongue

To winne silver, as he ful wel koude;
To win silver, as he knew full well how to do.

Therefore he song the murierly* and loude.   *more merrily
Therefore he sung more merrily and louder.

In this portrait, the last of the pilgrims to be described, Chaucer is absolutely uncompromising, in a way rarely found elsewhere in *The Canterbury Tales*. The Pardoner is a loathsome creature, physically repulsive and morally repugnant. His alliance with the Summoner is dubious — he rides with the Summoner, with whom he sings love songs. Chaucer's description of the Summoner has been equally damning, and the image is of a pair of scoundrels. Worse, the Pardoner's lack of manhood suggests that he is the passive partner in an abhorrent homosexual relationship with the Summoner.

The Pardoner's appearance is made revolting. He has lank yellow hair that is thinning, and which hangs down in rats'-tails over his shoulders. He tries to be fashionable, riding bare-headed apart from his religious cap, which has a religious relic pinned to it. He carries other relics and pardons with him. He has glaring eyes like a hare, and he has a tiny high voice and bleats like a goat. He also has no beard and is unlikely to ever have one, because (in the narrator's opinion) he is probably a castrato or even a woman. Despite this he sings and preaches well in church.

Although Chaucer says there is no other pardoner like him in the whole of England (itself a double-edged remark), his pre-eminence consists in his ability to dupe gullible people through his eloquence and with his false relics. He is a professional pardoner, and the Veronica on his cap advertises his trade. As well as his pardons (indulgences) he has a whole series of false relics, which he uses to trick people out of their money. He travels around, and when he arrives at a place he makes more money in one day than the parish priest can make in two months.

Chaucer does not prevaricate here; he exposes the Pardoner's corrupt practices right away and says that everything he offers is false. Chaucer makes it abundantly clear that the Pardoner is spiritually bankrupt, a defect mirrored by his apparent physical castration. Medieval people believed that a person's physical appearance was a reflection of their inner state. The Pardoner's disgusting appearance is a clear indicator of his spiritual corruption. He has no redeeming virtues, because although he sings and preaches well, these gifts are used entirely in the service of personal gain.

The Pardoner and the Church

There are two aspects to the Pardoner's work — the sale of indulgences, and the sale or use of holy relics.

Indulgences

Pardoners were licensed operatives employed by the Church to dispense indulgences. It is essential to be clear about how this system operated.

A Christian who committed sin, especially a mortal sin such as gluttony, needed to confess his sin to a priest in order to receive absolution. If he died before this spiritual cleansing took place, his soul would be eternally damned. Genuine repentance was necessary, whereupon a priest could grant absolution on Christ's behalf, and as it were wipe the slate clean. In order to signify that the sinner was truly repentant, he would normally undertake penance, commonly dictated by the priest. A simple sin might merely require the saying of some prayers as a penance, but penances could be considerable. Pilgrimages, for example, were sometimes undertaken as a form of penance, and could entail enormous inconvenience and expense.

The practice grew of allowing people to commute the penance required after confession, frequently by means of a payment. Pardoners were employed to provide indulgences, provided by a bishop or even by the Pope, remitting part or all of

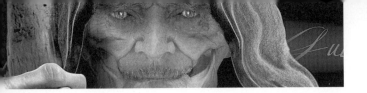

the imposed penance. These rapidly grew in popularity, but were open to abuse. A pardoner might offer forged indulgences. In more sinister fashion, people began to view indulgences as pardons for the sin rather than a remission of the penance, and corrupt pardoners were happy for this confusion to exist. Chaucer's Pardoner actually claims to be able to offer absolution, instead of merely offering indulgences.

Corrupt practices were known and condemned from an early stage. By the fourteenth century, the malpractices described by Chaucer were commonplace, and widely condemned. Chaucer's contemporary William Langland offers a very close parallel to 'The Pardoner's Prologue':

> There preched a pardonere as he a prest were,
> Broughte forth a bulle with bishopes seles,
> And seide that hymself mighte assoilen hem alle
> Of falshed of fastyng of vowes ybroken.
> Lewed men leved hym wel and lyked his wordes…
> Thus they geven here golde glotones to kepe.
>
> (*Piers Plowman*, B Text Prologue, lines 68–72, 76)

> *There preached a pardoner as if he were a priest;*
> *He brought out a licence with a bishop's seals,*
> *And claimed that he could absolve them all*
> *For failing in fasting or breaking vows.*
> *Ignorant people believed him well and liked his words…*
> *Thus they give their gold to gluttons.*

Eventually, anger against the false use of indulgences was a significant impetus for the Reformation in the sixteenth century.

Relics

The importance of relics in the medieval Catholic Church depends upon the basic Christian doctrine of the separation of the body and the soul. Sinful men could not plead directly to God because they were unworthy; they therefore needed to approach God by way of an intermediary. The Catholic priest performed this function, but there also existed all the saints — the pure and uncorrupted figures from the Church's history who had died without sin and therefore had privileged places next to God in Heaven. A sinful person on Earth could therefore invoke the assistance of a saint, hoping that they would intercede to God on the sinner's behalf. Although the souls of the saints were in Heaven, they had left their mortal bodies when they died, and so the bones of saints were highly venerated as relics of particular power. It was for this reason that saints' tombs — such as that of Saint Thomas Becket in Canterbury Cathedral — became major pilgrimage sites. Every Catholic altar contained the relics of a saint. Additionally, clothing or items that a saint had owned or touched would have holy attributes. Christ had been resurrected and ascended bodily to Heaven, but some of his blood had been spilt when he was nailed to the Cross, and the monastery of Hailes in Gloucestershire became widely famed for possessing a phial said to contain some of Christ's blood, a fact that Chaucer refers to in 'The Pardoner's Tale', line 366. The Pardoner himself claims to have a 'vernicle', a reproduction of the handkerchief with which Saint Veronica was supposed to have wiped Jesus' brow.

It is easy to see how such beliefs were open to abuse. An unscrupulous person could put forward any item and claim it as a holy relic. The Pardoner does exactly this, and confesses it openly to the pilgrims:

> Thanne shewe I forth my longe cristal stones,
> Ycrammed ful of cloutes and of bones —
> Relikes been they, as wenen they echoon.   ('The Pardoner's Prologue', lines 61–63)

'The General Prologue' has already made clear the falseness of the Pardoner's relics, for example the pillow-case that he says is the Virgin Mary's veil, and the pigs' bones he displays in a glass case.

There is ample evidence that all the abuses that Chaucer attributes to the Pardoner were known to be commonplace in fourteenth-century England. For example, the contemporary *Fasciculus Morum*, a fourteenth-century handbook for preachers, refers to false pardoners who used animal bones instead of real relics. The *Memoriale Presbiterorum*, another fourteenth-century handbook for the guidance of clergy, contains specific comments about exactly the false claims that the Pardoner makes. Everything that Chaucer writes would have been instantly recognisable to his audience.

'The Pardoner's Prologue and Tale'

'The Pardoner's Prologue'

Apart from the Wife of Bath, the Pardoner is the only pilgrim to whom Chaucer grants an extended personal prologue. This point is worthy of consideration early on because it suggests the care with which Chaucer builds up the significance of the Pardoner within *The Canterbury Tales*. The character, which is vividly established in 'The General Prologue', is developed at length in the Pardoner's own description of himself in his prologue. By the time we get to his tale, the character of the narrator has been fully delineated.

The Pardoner's prologue is in the form of a confession, a *confessio* in Latin. This was a conventional literary form, where a character reveals his true nature through self-confession. The immediate model for Chaucer's Pardoner seems to have been the character of Faux-Semblant (False Seeming) in the long French poem *La Roman de la Rose*, part of which Chaucer translated into English. The unrealistic and formal nature of the *confessio* is contrasted with the naturalistic manner and speech of the Pardoner.

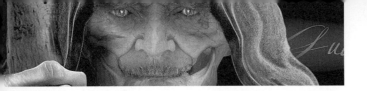

Additionally, the prologue introduces the characteristic medieval sermon form, which starts with a statement of the 'theme' in Latin, is amplified through citation of authorities and the use of an *exemplum* (example), and concludes with a recapitulation of the main point. In the Pardoner's case the parts are spread between the prologue and his story of the three rioters, essentially giving 'The Pardoner's Prologue and Tale' an artistic unity. In his prologue the Pardoner explains his preaching technique, and how he begins with the statement of the 'theme', '*Radix malorum est Cupiditas*' (line 48) — 'the love of money is the root of all evil'.

Lines 43–48

The Pardoner immediately proclaims that he is a performer:

> I peyne me to han an hauteyn speche (line 44)

He admits that he only ever has one topic when he preaches:

> *Radix malorum est Cupiditas.* (line 48)

The irony of this will become apparent as his confession continues.

Lines 49–54

He begins his sermons by showing his licence to preach, in order to protect himself, 'my body to warente' (line 52). So far there is no suggestion that he is anything other than a legitimate pardoner, undertaking the Church's work.

Lines 55–60

He softens up his audience by speaking Latin (line 58). This makes him sound authoritative. His audience would associate a Latin speaker with a clergyman — someone wise whom they were used to obeying.

Lines 61–65

The first part of his repertoire is the 'holy' relics he shows — but he already confesses that these are fakes:

> Relikes been they, as wenen they echoon. (line 63)

He clearly does not intend to maintain a pretence of honesty or legitimacy.

Lines 66–90

The Pardoner explains the claims he makes for the miraculous powers of his 'relics'. Given the admission in line 63, the hollowness of the claims is apparent, but similar claims were sincerely made by the Church for thousands of relics during the Middle Ages. The end of the section is marked by the sinister mention of monetary gain:

> So that he offre pens, or elles grotes. (line 90)

The link back to line 48 is clear. The Pardoner preaches that men should part with their money, but he is the one who accumulates it.

Lines 91–102

This is the Pardoner's cynical disclaimer that a sinner will have no power to make a true offering. He thus protects himself against claims that his relics do not work. He can retort that their failure must be due to the sinful state of the person concerned.

Lines 103–08

This is open confession, and a boast. The Pardoner boasts about the amount of money he has gained — a hundred marks a year, a huge sum — through his false practices, 'this gaude' (line 103).

Lines 109–16

He explains his preaching technique, with the immensely visual image of a dove sitting on a barn and stretching out its neck. His confession deepens with the admission that he uses 'an hundred false japes moore' (line 108). He boasts of his own skill:

> Mine handes and my tonge goon so yerne
> That it is joye to se my bisynesse.   (lines 112–13)

The admission of his own avarice is blatant now, with the ironic statement that although he preaches against avarice, his intention is 'to make hem free / To yeven hir pens, and namely unto me' (lines 115–16).

Lines 117–36

At this point the malignant nature of the Pardoner is truly shown. In a Christian world where the salvation of the soul was the first priority, he is willing to condemn his listeners to eternal damnation provided that he gains money from them:

> For myn entente is nat but for to winne,
> And nothing for correccioun of sinne.
> I rekke nevere, whan that they been beried,
> Though that hir soules goon a-blakeberied.   (lines 117–20)

This is where the literary form of the *confessio* is most at odds with the naturalistic nature of the writing; the Pardoner's self-awareness and willingness to confess his depravity seems unlikely. Chaucer offers a picture of literary **hubris**, the arrogance that courts disaster.

He continues by focusing on those who have attacked him or his fellow pardoners — these people he will openly defame. Again, he openly admits his hypocrisy and depths of his malignancy, comparing himself to a venomous snake:

> Thus spitte I out my venym under hewe
> Of hoolinesse, to semen hooly and trewe.   (lines 135–36)

The snake image suggests that he is like Satan, who also used words deceitfully to tempt Adam and Eve. A modern audience might be reminded of Iago in *Othello*.

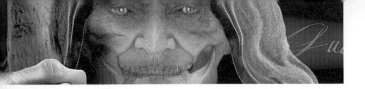

Lines 137–48

He reiterates his opening statements, with the addition of the paradox of which he is fully aware:

> Thus kan I preche again that same vice
> Which that I use, and that is avarice. (lines 141–42)

This degree of self-awareness may be unrealistic, but Chaucer is making a profound point about the depth of evil which the Pardoner represents. It is hard to see how the point could be more dramatically achieved than through the form of the *confessio*.

Lines 149–67

The Pardoner freely confesses that there is no boundary to his desire for money and possessions, and no moral scruple that holds him back from their acquisition:

> I wol have moneie, wolle, chese, and whete,
> Al were it yeven of the povereste page,
> Or of the povereste widwe in a village (lines 162–64)

If not before, the Pardoner here becomes a loathsome creature, willing to take money from the very poorest people in society, and willing to admit that he does so.

Lines 168–76

Having concluded at this nadir, the Pardoner offers to begin his actual tale. Before he does so there is a further paradox, which once again he fully understands:

> For though myself be a ful vicious man,
> A moral tale yet I yow telle kan (lines 173–74)

The fascination of the Pardoner for many readers is how a man of such apparent insight and self-awareness can be so morally bankrupt. It is Chaucer's craft to make the revelations of this 'ful vicious man' seem somehow credible.

'The Pardoner's Tale'

The story that the Pardoner tells acts as an *exemplum* — a moral example or story that exemplifies a theme. The Pardoner's theme, as stated in his prologue, is that '*Radix malorum est Cupiditas*' (line 48) — 'the love of money is the root of all evil'. His story is an *exemplum* for this text, showing how 'Cupiditas' destroys the three revellers. It does not simply do this, however. It links a number of sins together and binds them to the character of the revellers, so that their avarice is seen as just one aspect of their overall corruption and sinfulness. At the end of the story the Pardoner reverts to addressing the pilgrims directly.

Lines 177–96

The Pardoner introduces the revellers in a general way as a 'compaignye' (line 177) of dissolute young men, guilty of numerous vices and several of the deadly sins. They are sinners and blasphemers:

> Oure blissed Lordes body they totere (line 188)

Although this may not seem too terrible to a modern reader, a medieval audience would have recognised this as being at the most dreadful end of the spectrum of sin. Nor do they repent:

> And ech of hem at otheres sinne lough. (line 190)

Already they deserve to be damned for the extent of the sins.

Before continuing with the story, the Pardoner introduces an apparent digression in lines 197–374. This has two functions. It has the dramatic function of delaying the story proper, which maintains tension and expectation. More importantly, it has the thematic function of enlarging on the nature of various kinds of sin, linking them all together in a picture of human depravity. This makes the ensuing story more hard-hitting, and impacts more fully on the Pardoner's audience — whom he will later ask for money.

Lines 197–262

The first sin the Pardoner addresses is gluttony. This was one of the seven deadly sins, which meant that a person guilty of it would face eternal damnation. In common with medieval practice, the Pardoner adduces several examples to illustrate the point. Intriguingly (to modern minds) he suggests that Adam's fault was gluttony. This is understandable if it is remembered that in medieval minds all the sins were linked, and all contributed to the chief sin of pride. Adam's eating of the apple is seen as the willingness to put bodily satisfaction before spiritual well-being; the severity of this sin, which might appear relatively minor to a modern mind familiar to the idea of over-consumption, is spelt out strikingly at the end of this section:

> But certes, he that haunteth swiche delices
> Is deed, whil that he liveth in tho vices. (lines 261–62)

Lines 263–302

The Pardoner moves seamlessly from a denunciation of gluttony in general to deal with the issue of drunkenness in particular. Again his condemnation is trenchant, and in this case the modern reader may more easily recognise the problem:

> For dronkenesse is verray sepulture
> Of mannes wit and his discrecioun. (lines 272–73)

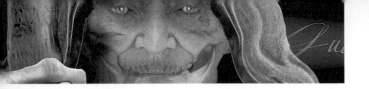

Lines 303–42

The Pardoner moves on to deal with gambling. This may seem unconnected, but it is one of the vices that is identified at the beginning of the tale, and all the sins he describes — gluttony, drunkenness, gambling, swearing — are specifically associated with the three rioters who will shortly become the focus of the story. As usual, specific *exempla* are used to illustrate the sin.

Lines 343–74

The last section of the digression is devoted to swearing, which takes the form of blasphemy. As stated above, this is seen as the most terrible of all behaviours, because it is a direct attack on God. The language is uncompromising:

> Lo, rather he forbedeth swich swering
> Than homicide or many a cursed thing   (lines 357–58)

The Pardoner builds up this section to a declaration that links the sins together and suggests that murder is an inevitable outcome — as it will be in the story:

> This fruit cometh of the bicched bones two,
> Forswering, ire, falsnesse, homicide.   (lines 370–71)

The anger (ire) mentioned in line 371 is another of the seven deadly sins, and will be immediately associated with the three rioters as they begin their quest 'al dronken in this rage' (line 419). At the end of his tale, the Pardoner too will give way to anger when the Host confronts him (line 671).

Lines 375–405

Abruptly, the Pardoner returns to his story, keeping the audience on their toes by his changes of pace and subject. He re-starts the story with a neat trick, making it seem that the audience are familiar with the protagonists who have not in fact been previously singled out from the gang of revellers at the beginning of his tale:

> Thise riotoures thre of whiche I telle.   (line 375)

This saves time and engages the audience instantly in the story. The fact that they are already drinking in the inn before dawn, 'long erst er prime' (line 376), is a link to the 'digression' which has spelt out the evils of drunkenness.

Hard against this, the Pardoner introduces the subject of death, first in the death of one of their fellows, and then in the sinister shape of Death itself, personified and given physical presence by the innkeeper and the servant:

> Ther cam a privee theef men clepeth Deeth,
> That in this contree al the peple sleeth.   (line 389–90)

There is black humour here for the audience, which is about to be intensified.

Lines 406–24

The rioters' absurd oath to kill Death is introduced by the kind of blasphemy that the Pardoner has already identified as particularly hideous:

> Ye, Goddes armes! (line 406)

The Pardoner emphasises the point:

> And many a grisly ooth thanne han they sworn,
> And Cristes blessed body al torente (lines 422–23)

He ends the section with another portentous and darkly humorous line in which the word 'if' is crucial:

> Deeth shal be deed, if that they may him hente. (line 424)

Lines 425–52

The story of the three rioters is told with remarkable economy. The rioters have hardly begun their quest when they encounter a mysterious old man, whose nature is deliberately left vague. The rioters are too blind to perceive anything other than his age, and although he greets them meekly they are instantly abusive, in accordance with the characteristics the Pardoner has set up for them:

> Why livestow so longe in so greet age? (line 433)

The old man's memorable and resonant reply that he cannot find anybody 'that wolde chaunge his youthe for myn age' (line 438) should be sufficient rebuke, but the rioters are impervious.

Lines 453–73

The old man continues to speak politely and ask them to behave courteously, but the rioters remain abusive. They accuse him of being in league with Death:

> For soothly thou art oon of his assent
> To sleen us yonge folk, thou false theef! (lines 472–73)

The irony of this is clear — the rioters will surely find death, whether the old man directs them or not.

Lines 474–89

The old man's reply crackles with contempt disguised by meekness:

> 'Now, sires,' quod he, 'if that yow be so leef
> To finde Deeth, turne up this croked wey' (lines 474–75)

In terms of the story this is intriguing, for the audience as well as the young men. What will they find? The fact that the old man left Death there means that he is unaffected by whatever lies under the tree.

There is no drawn-out tension here. In keeping with the general economy of the story, it is immediately revealed that the rioters discover a heap of gold. The irony of death taking this form is not lost on the audience, although it completely escapes the young men themselves. The audience will also note the irony that an obsession with money leads directly to death, yet the Pardoner has confessed to exactly that kind of avarice.

Lines 490–519

'The worste' (line 490) of the rioters takes the lead, claiming that they will carry the treasure away by night, and immediately hatching a plan to send the youngest away. Again he is blind to what is happening:

> This tresor hath Fortune unto us yiven,
> In mirthe and joliftee oure lyf to liven.   (lines 493–94)

The 'tresor' will be a painful death, and is not a result of luck, but of their own choices.

Lines 520–50

The two elder rioters plot to kill the third. They are still oblivious to what is happening here; the audience is well aware of where this is leading.

Lines 551–92

Inevitably, the youngest man plots to kill the other two. The Pardoner makes explicit the fact that he (and they) deserve to die because of their sinfulness:

> For-why the feend foond him in swich livinge
> That he hadde leve him to sorwe bringe.   (lines 561–62)

In line 582 refers to him simply as 'this cursed man' — a murderer, like Cain.

Lines 593–602

The finale of the tale is the briefest of all the sections, emphasising its inevitability. The Pardoner unceremoniously records the death of the rioters in ten stark lines.

> What nedeth it to sermone of it moore?   (line 593)

Lines 603–17

Balanced against the terseness of the story's ending is the way the Pardoner dwells on the hideous and painful death caused by the poison, and then finishes with a rhetorical flourish against all the sins he has enumerated.

Lines 618–29

In a sudden switch of tone the Pardoner appeals directly to the audience of his sermon, and in the wake of the powerful story he is able to claim the power to grant absolution, which was reserved for priests:

> I yow assoille by myn heigh power   (line 627)

— provided they offer him money.

Lines 629–54

It comes as something of a shock to the modern reader, and presumably to Chaucer's audience, to be reminded in line 629 that they are not being addressed directly, but are hearing second-hand an example of the sermons the Pardoner preaches. Such has been the narrative skill that we forget that circumstance, and the Pardoner strikingly switches back to direct address in the middle of a line. The depth of his cunning (or self-deception) is revealed when he now attempts to play the identical trick on the pilgrims as he has used on his sermon's audience. He relies on the force of his words and the tale he has told to carry him through, and persuade the pilgrims themselves to buy his pardons. He harps on their fears, as any skilful insurance salesman would do:

> Paraventure ther may fallen oon or two
> Doun of his hors, and breke his nekke atwo. (lines 649–50)

Chaucer's audience, and the modern reader, are left to wonder whether this brazen approach will succeed. The power of the Pardoner's theme, *Radix malorum est Cupiditas*, is now doubly striking as his avarice manifests itself.

Lines 655–82

It would seem that his choice of the Host is a masterstroke, because the Host is known to react with ready feeling and without an intellectual response. But Chaucer has a major twist to add, and ends the tale with wild humour. The Host's scathing denunciation of the Pardoner silences him, and exposes all his cheap tricks as exactly that — cheap. The moral force of the Pardoner's story is not lessened, but rather increased by the awareness that the Pardoner is as likely to be damned as the rioters.

There is an irony too in the Pardoner's choice of the Host as the most gullible pilgrim. The Host is in charge of the story-telling 'game' that the pilgrims are using to pass the time on the journey, and he has offered a free meal for the best story he hears on the pilgrimage. If the Pardoner had hoped to impress the Host and win the meal, he is rudely awakened here.

It is worth noting that the end of 'The Pardoner's Tale' is also the end of one of the sequences in the manuscripts. There is no indication of whose tale was meant to follow this one, and no conclusions can be drawn about Chaucer's intentions or scheme.

Gothic and macabre elements

One of the most noticeable aspects of 'The Pardoner's Prologue and Tale' is its preoccupation with death, both in the tale of the rioters and in the context of the vocation of the Pardoner, who offers a kind of insurance to people against the mortal consequence of their sins. For this reason the text has been described as 'Gothic'.

This term 'Gothic' sits awkwardly in a discussion of Chaucer. It was invented to describe the genre of eighteenth- and nineteenth-century novels that were set in the

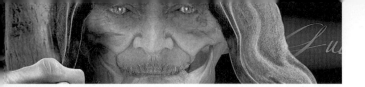

Middle Ages (the Gothic period of art and architecture), and which featured an obsession with the supernatural and macabre, death in relation to these, and frequently the depiction of an unhealthy or abnormal psychological state. It is therefore a historical term, dependent on a backward-looking view of the Middle Ages, rather than one that can be applied directly to medieval literature. It is easy, however, to see how the term can be retrospectively applied to elements of 'The Pardoner's Tale', which shows the kind of obsessions that Gothic writers emphasised.

The word 'macabre' literally means 'gruesome', particularly in the sense of being associated with death. The word comes from the French *Danse Macabre*, the 'Dance of Death', which was a common subject in medieval art and literature. The word has particular relevance to 'The Pardoner's Tale', which has death as a recurrent theme.

The macabre

The emphasis on death is clear throughout. Centrally there is the rioters' quest for Death, which ends with their grisly demise at each other's hands. Framing the whole of 'The Pardoner's Prologue and Tale' there is the Pardoner's reminder that all the pilgrims are only a step away from death at any moment:

> Paraventure ther may fallen oon or two
> Doun of his hors, and breke his nekke atwo.   (lines 649–50)

For a medieval person to die in a state of mortal sin would mean eternal damnation of the soul. In this context, the Pardoner's preaching and the Pardoner's story are meant to be disquieting and disturbing, making his audiences feel more vulnerable and therefore more likely to purchase his services. Every sin dwelt on by the Pardoner or committed by the rioters is intended to emphasise the importance of seeking salvation by any means rather than go to Hell. The willingness of the Pardoner to let such damnation happen is deeply repulsive:

> I rekke nevere, whan that they been beried,
> Though that hir soules goon a-blakeberied.   (lines 119–20)

The audience's awareness of the Pardoner's own damned state adds a further macabre element to these lines, and to the tone of the whole work.

The emphasis on bodily corruption

This aspect of the macabre resonates throughout 'The Pardoner's Prologue and Tale'. The link between the revellers' abuse of their own bodies and their 'tearing' of Christ's body through blasphemy is very strong. Medieval Christianity emphasised the distinction between the body and the soul, and the purpose of Christian living was to purify the soul for eternal life. The revellers gorge themselves with meat and drink, which the Pardoner terms 'cursed superfluitee' (line 242). The image that when a man gets drunk 'of his throte he maketh his privee' (line 241) is deliberately repulsive. The long description of the cooks' endeavours to make gluttony pleasant and easy (lines 252–60) is linked to the hideous description of the stomach as 'Fulfilled of dong and of corrupcioun' (line 249). The rioters start drunk (line 377) and end up dying from poisoned drink (lines 599–602). It is impossible to forget that the Pardoner has demanded food and drink himself before he begins his tale. In this context the attribution of Adam's fall to gluttony (lines 219–21) seems justifiable, because through eating the forbidden fruit his body becomes corrupted.

The references to tearing Christ's body have already been mentioned (e.g. lines 188–89), but there are other aspects of bodily corruption. The old man is described as wasting away (line 446), and crucially the Pardoner himself is described as possibly a eunuch in 'The General Prologue'. Even so, the Host offers to castrate him at the end of the tale, as a final thematic reminder of the deformed state of corrupted bodies and souls.

The supernatural

To a modern audience, the whole of 'The Pardoner's Prologue and Tale' can seem to be imbued with the supernatural, in the form of the relics and promises that the Pardoner makes. However, a medieval audience would have taken these as spiritual matters, rather than supernatural in the modern sense. The truly supernatural figure in 'The Pardoner's Tale' is the old man whom the rioters meet. However he is interpreted, he seems to have more than natural qualities. He explains that although he wishes to die, he cannot. In a more sinister fashion, he claims to know Death, and to have left him shortly before he encounters the rioters. He is able to direct them towards Death:

> For in that grove I lafte him, by my fey (line 476)

The personification of Death

The **personification** of Death in the tale is at once comic and disturbing. The introduction of him by the servant as an apparently real person is darkly humorous:

> Ther cam a privee theef men clepeth Deeth,
> That in this contree al the peple sleeth (lines 389–90)

But the next reference is more sinister, when the innkeeper confirms that:

> ...he hath slain this yeer
> Henne over a mile, withinne a greet village,
> Bothe man and womman, child, and hine, and page (lines 400–02)

The reference to the Black Death is unmistakable, with the indiscriminate and inexorable slaughter of whole populations. There is an unpleasant frisson in the assertion that:

> I trowe his habitacioun be there.   (line 403)

Here Death takes on a more substantial presence, which renders the audience more uneasy at the same time that it makes the rioter's defiance more absurd:

> Is it swich peril with him for to meete?   (line 407)

To an audience with immediate memories of the Black Death, such bravado would seem grotesque.

The unnerving quality of the depiction of Death reaches its height with the old man's claim to know Death and to have left him in a grove, as mentioned above. 'Left' can mean 'parted from', but it can also mean that the old man has deliberately placed Death in the grove (in the form of the coins), and the personification finally receives a concrete form. Terror might be too strong a word for a modern audience, but the sense of fear and unease that would be engendered in a medieval audience accustomed to the permanent proximity of death is easy to recognise.

The attractiveness of evil as personified in the Pardoner

Despite, or perhaps because of, his personal grotesqueness, his complete hypocrisy and his unprincipled misuse of his position, the Pardoner remains a fascinating character, and this is a typically Gothic theme. He offers a vicarious insight into a twisted and tortured soul, preaching every day against sin and warning of its eternal consequences, while indulging in precisely the sins he is talking about.

Literature is full of evil figures who seem more interesting than good characters. Satan as portrayed by Milton, Iago in *Othello*, Alex in *A Clockwork Orange* — throughout history authors (and audiences) have been fascinated by the motivations of apparently entirely wicked characters, and it is worth comparing the Pardoner with others in order to consider common features. Daring against odds, panache and style, eloquence and often humour are all elements that can turn the grotesque into the absorbing. True Gothic texts like *Frankenstein* and *Dracula* offer good points of comparison.

The Pardoner's uncertain sexuality equally has a Gothic resonance. Chaucer the Pilgrim believes him to be 'a gelding or a mare' ('The General Prologue', line 693), while he apparently sings love duets with the Summoner ('The General Prologue', lines 674–75). This suggestion of homosexuality or emasculation offers ample scope for a modern reader to develop all kinds of theories about the Pardoner's psychological state, which would help to explain his otherwise extraordinary self-exposure. In medieval terms, his latent homosexuality would be a perversion, suggesting the unredeemed corruption of the body. He is outside society, almost outside nature, and so he has little to lose by preying on ordinary men and women.

Characters

The rioters and the old man

Part of the power of 'The Pardoner's Tale' is that it is simultaneously naturalistic and evidently symbolic. Chaucer's writing gives it a naturalistic feel; the quest for Death indicates that we are to look for symbolic meaning throughout.

This is very evident when we look at the main characters — the three rioters, and the old man they meet. In each case there is a range of interpretations that are worth exploring.

The rioters: possible interpretations

Individuals

Chaucer takes great care to make the rioters seem like ordinary people. Their speech is **colloquial**:

> Ey! Goddes precious dignitee! who wende
> To-day that we sholde han so fair a grace? (lines 496–97)

and they behave like ordinary friends:

> Herkneth, felawes, we thre been al ones;
> Lat ech of us holde up his hand til oother
> And ech of us bicomen otheres brother (lines 410–12)

Their drunken boast that they will kill Death is all too human:

> He shal be slain, he that so manye sleeth,
> By Goddes dignitee, er it be night. (lines 414–15)

A trinity

The fact that there are three rioters adds an ominous layer of symbolism to the tale. To a Christian mind, the number three is inescapably linked with the Holy Trinity — God the Father, God the Son and God the Holy Ghost. The rioters instantly form a kind of anti-trinity. They mock the true Trinity through their blasphemy; they mock it through their treachery and betrayal of each other. In a simpler sense, a trio of friends or siblings is a traditional feature of folk tales and fairy stories, and allows conflict where two gang up against the third (who in this case ironically defeats them).

Sinners

In the context of the Pardoner's digression on sin, lines 197–374, it is clear that we are to take the rioters as being representative of sinful men:

> They daunce and pleyen at dees bothe day and night,
> And eten also and drinken over hir might (lines 181–82)

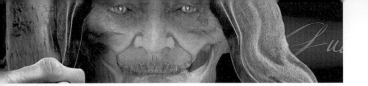

> Hir othes been so grete and so dampnable
> That it is grisly for to heere hem swere.　　　　　　　(lines 186–87)

They are also so steeped in sin that the devil may easily tempt them to murder:

> And atte laste the feend, oure enemy,
> Putte in his thought that he sholde poison beye　　　(lines 558–59)

The Pardoner's final rhetorical flourish confirms that the rioters are archetypally sinners:

> O cursed sinne of alle cursednesse!
> O traitours homicide, O wikkednesse!　　　　　　　(lines 609–10)

All of us

To the medieval mind, all men are sinners, because all share in the Original Sin of Adam and Eve, from which Christ redeemed mankind. It is simple to see, therefore, that the Pardoner's audience were expected to perceive in his sermon faults that they might easily be guilty of themselves. That is why he can move directly from his tale of the revellers to the sins of his auditors:

> Now, goode men, God foryeve yow youre trespas,
> And ware yow fro the sinne of avarice!　　　　　　　(lines 618–19)

The first line has its direct reference to the Lord's Prayer, 'forgive us our trespasses', in which all Christians admit their sinful nature, before the Pardoner focuses specifically on the deadly sin of avarice (it should be noted that the reference to 'goode men' in line 618 is mere politeness, like 'gentlemen', and does not imply that the audience are morally good). It may take a little effort for a modern audience, not necessarily Christian and not necessarily brought up with a notion of universal sinfulness, to reconstruct the mindset of the original audiences for the Pardoner's sermon, both fictitious and real. It is necessary, however, to realise the significance of the point, because it is on this basis that the Pardoner can justify offering his pardons and relics to a believing audience.

The old man: possible interpretations

An individual

As with the rioters, Chaucer paints a vivid picture. The old man responds to the oafishness of the rioters politely and with dignity:

> But sires, to yow it is no curteisye
> To speken to an old man vileynye　　　　　　　　　(lines 453–54)

At the same time the irony of his response is clear when they abusively ask him why he is still alive:

> For I ne kan nat finde / A man…
> That wolde chaunge his youthe for myn age.' (lines 435–36, 438)

Old age/mortality

He is described as 'an oold man' (line 427) as soon as the rioters meet him, but the symbolic representation is confirmed later:

> Lo how I vanisshe, flessh and blood and skin!
> Allas! Whan shul my bones been at reste? (lines 446–47)

Even more striking is the image of him knocking on the ground, seeking to die:

> And on the ground, which is my moodres gate,
> I knokke with my staf, bothe erly and late,
> And seye, "Leeve mooder, leet me in!" (lines 443–45)

The voice of wisdom

There is an important and simple distinction between the 'old man' and the 'yonge folk that haunteden folye' (line 178). It was conventional that old age brought wisdom, and that young people should listen to their elders. It is perhaps equally conventional that the young people pay no attention. The old man speaks politely to them and tells them only the truth, but they abuse him and ignore what he says. It is only when they persist in their folly that he points the way to death.

The Wandering Jew

There was a very popular medieval legend about the Wandering Jew. The exact origins of the legend are debatable, but concern a figure, perhaps a man who insulted Jesus on the way to his Crucifixion, who was cursed and doomed to remain alive and wander the Earth to await the Second Coming of Christ.

There is no direct suggestion in 'The Pardoner's Tale' that the old man represents the Wandering Jew, but Chaucer may have taken from a current popular legend the powerful image of a cursed man who wants to die but cannot do so.

Death's accomplice

This is the easiest association to find:

> 'Now, sires,' quod he, 'if that yow be so leef
> To finde Deeth, turne up this croked wey,
> For in that grove I lafte him, by my fey' (lines 474–76)

He directs the rioters to their death, knowing full well what will happen if they turn onto the 'croked wey'. However, it should be noted that he only says this after they have provoked and abused him. In line 463 he intends to leave without giving them directions.

Death

This is just an extension of the previous interpretation, and rests on the same evidence. Death was conventionally represented in art as a male hooded skeleton figure, so a skeletal-looking old man would be a near image. If the old man represents mortality anyway, it is easy to visualise the macabre image of a death figure pointing the way to death itself.

The Devil

The old man manifestly tempts the rioters into mortal sin. He points the way to them, and states that it is a 'croked wey', the path of sin. The image is strongly biblical — Paul in the Acts of the Apostles (Chapter 13, verse 10) accuses the sorcerer Elymas of making crooked the straight ways of the Lord. The Pardoner's (and Chaucer's) audiences would have been in no doubt about the symbolic force of the image. The old man sits beside a stile (line 426), which symbolically represents a decision point. The rioters turn aside from the true way and rush to their deaths.

Gullible characters

The Pardoner's success depends on his ability to make people believe what he says, that is to say on their degree of credulity or gullibility. This idea becomes one of Chaucer's central concerns in 'The Pardoner's Prologue and Tale'. Being Chaucer, he examines the issue from several angles.

The rioters in 'The Pardoner's Tale'

The rioters are easily deceived. Despite being warned by the serving-boy about the danger of meeting Death, the rioters are contemptuous:

> Is it swich peril with him for to meete? (line 407)

This classic example of a rhetorical question shows the depth of the rioters' ignorance and arrogance. When the old man directs them up the 'croked wey', they rush off to meet their death without a thought, unaware of the distinction between the appearance of the situation and its reality.

The Pardoner's usual audience

A similar failure characterises the usual audience for one of the Pardoner's sermons, but at least they have an excuse. They fear for their immortal souls, and knowing themselves sinners it is natural that they should seek redemption for their actions, and even insurance for what they might do. Blessed relics, they believed, had holy powers and could cure ills and protect them:

> Taak water of that welle and wassh his tonge,
> And it is hool anon. (lines 70–71)

Indulgences could alleviate the punishment for their sins, or even excuse them from punishment altogether:

> Myn hooly pardoun may yow alle warice. (line 620)

When the soul is at stake, it is understandable that people would clutch at the opportunities the Pardoner offers them. Their failure to consider whether the Pardoner's claims are genuine is forgivable.

The Pardoner himself

Thus far people's gullibility is straightforward, motivated by pride (in the case of the rioters) or fear (in the case of the Pardoner's normal audience). Chaucer extends the theme, however, by making the Pardoner himself fallible. For some reason — arguably through pride — the Pardoner believes he can dupe the pilgrims to whom he has just made his confession. He too fails to distinguish the true situation. He believes that the Host is gullible enough to fall for his tricks, even after he has exposed the mechanism. That he is dumbfounded by the Host's retort is evident:

> This Pardoner answerde nat a word;
> So wrooth he was, no word ne wolde he seye. (lines 670–71)

The Canterbury pilgrims

It is Chaucer's irony that makes the pilgrims the clear-sighted figures in 'The Pardoner's Tale'. If the Host, amongst the most literal and least perceptive of the pilgrims, can see through the Pardoner's attempt to con him so easily, then we are meant to understand that the pilgrims are sophisticated enough to distinguish truth from lies, unlike the Pardoner's usual audiences. This is not lessened by the Pardoner's earlier confession — he still attempts to dupe them at the end. The reaction of the pilgrims is the worst reaction the Pardoner can receive — 'al the peple lough' (line 675) at him. This is the nature of Chaucer's satire — exposing folly and vice through laughter at it.

Chaucer's audience

By extension, Chaucer's audience vicariously share in the Host's scathing denunciation of the Pardoner. This makes them feel superior, in that they too have not been deceived by the Pardoner's tricks, and can laugh at the gullibility of others. They appreciate in full Chaucer's satirical intent, and the way that the Pardoner's hollowness has been exposed.

The Host and the Pardoner

The Host has a crucial role in any analysis of the Pardoner, because his comments form a frame within which ' The Pardoner's Prologue and Tale' take place and are judged. Prior to the Pardoner's prologue comes its introduction, forming a bridge

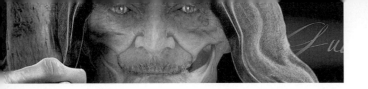

between the previous (Physician's) tale and the Pardoner's contribution. The introduction consists of the Host's response to 'The Physician's Tale', followed by him calling on the Pardoner to tell the pilgrims some 'mirthe or japes' (line 33). At the end of 'The Pardoner's Tale', the Pardoner famously calls on the Host to come forward first because he is 'moost envoluped in sinne' (line 656). The Host's reply forms the conclusion of 'The Pardoner's Prologue and Tale'.

The Host in the Introduction to 'The Pardoner's Prologue and Tale'

The Pardoner is preceded in *The Canterbury Tales* by a doctor, who tells 'The Physician's Tale'. This is a very short story (286 lines) about a beautiful maiden named Virginia who accepts death (at her father's hand) rather than having to lose her virginity to an evil man who has conspired against her.

The Host, whose name is Harry Bailly, responds to 'The Physician's Tale' with ready humanity and sympathy. He feels as much for the fictional characters depicted in it as he does for real people. He lacks critical perceptiveness and acuity — he tends to take things at face value. He feels strong sympathy for the innocent girl: 'Allas, so pitously as she was slain!' (line 12), and similarly strong condemnation of the guilty individuals: 'This was a fals cherl and a fals justise' (line 3). He freely admits this emotional response: 'But wel I woot thou doost myn herte to erme' (line 26), and that unless there is a remedy 'Myn herte is lost for pitee of this maide' (line 31). It may be this simplicity that causes the Pardoner to choose him as a target at the end of his tale.

The choice of the Pardoner as the next story-teller

It is evident from 'The General Prologue' that the Pardoner is a grotesque figure. The Host presumably wishes to follow a sad tale with something cheerful from a man who rides along singing love songs with his friend the Summoner, and who is clearly a regular drinker. He specifically asks for 'som mirthe or japes right anon' (line 33).

Chaucer's purpose is uncertain, given the fragmentary nature of *The Canterbury Tales*, but the two tales seem to share a moral purpose, although very differently delivered. It can easily be argued, however, that Chaucer wishes to continuously vary the tone of *The Canterbury Tales* by juxtaposing very different types of story and storyteller. It is worth noting that he defeats any expectation the audience may have of 'mirthe or japes', for the Pardoner's tale is a macabre one.

The Host at the end of 'The Pardoner's Tale'

The Pardoner seriously misjudges the Host at the end of his tale. He seems to think that, because the Host takes things literally and does not see the more sophisticated moral significance of what he hears, he will overlook the Pardoner's confession of his own corruption. The outcome is wildly comic. The Host is not nearly as limited as the Pardoner thinks, and responds violently to the Pardoner's suggestion that he is the most sinful of the pilgrims. His anger manifests in the most direct fashion, with a graphically vivid insult:

> I wolde I hadde thy coillons in myn hond
> In stide of relikes or of seintuarie.
> Lat kutte hem of, I wol thee helpe hem carie;
> They shul be shrined in an hogges toord! (lines 666–69)

The scathing brutality of this renders the Pardoner speechless, itself a surprise event. The Host has recognised the falsehood of the Pardoner's relics and his claims. Additionally, he seems to have picked up on the pilgrim Chaucer's suggestion that the Pardoner may be a eunuch — the suggestion of cutting off his testicles is doubly abusive when it appears that the Pardoner may not have any. The **parody** of religious ceremony, with the suggestion of treating the testicles as relics themselves, 'shrined in an hogges toord', is brazen and comical, especially as it reduces the eloquent Pardoner to silence:

> So wrooth he was, no word ne wolde he seye. (line 671)

It is salutary to note that the rhetorical and verbal sophistication of the Pardoner has been completely undone by the Host's coarse vocabulary — 'coillons', 'toord'. His earthy rejoinder invites the audience to consider its own response to the Pardoner and what he has to say.

'A ful vicious man'

At the end of his prologue the Pardoner states a paradox about his tale:

> For though myself be a ful vicious man,
> A moral tale yet I yow telle kan. (lines 173–74)

This is straightforward enough. A story can be independent of its narrator, and its moral worth is not connected to the virtue of its teller. But there is much more to 'The Pardoner's Prologue and Tale' than this. In his prologue the Pardoner has shown how he uses such tales to gain money — he has already shown that he is corrupt before he narrates his tale. Yet once it is finished, he encourages the pilgrims to buy his wares as if the confession in his prologue had never taken place.

It is worth remembering that 'vicious' should not be taken in its simple modern sense. Here it means, precisely, 'subject to or full of vice' — particularly those vices amongst the seven deadly sins of which the Pardoner is most guilty: pride, avarice, gluttony, anger and lechery.

The Pardoner's confession in lines 143–45 and 173–74

There are alternative responses. One can admire and sympathise with the self-awareness of a man who knows that he is wicked, and who yet achieves good ends

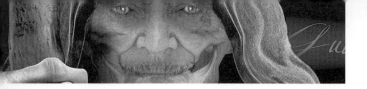

in spite of his own character. This seems to be the case in lines 143–45, because the Pardoner specifically says that he is able to make people turn away from avarice, despite recognising the sin in himself.

However, the Pardoner who advances this line of reasoning also rejects it. In lines 117–18 he states:

> For myn entente is nat but for to winne,
> And nothing for correccioun of sinne.

That is to say, he realises that his sermons may have the effect of turning people from sin, but this is not his intention. He does not care about their souls any more than his own, and is happy for them to be damned:

> I rekke nevere, whan that they been beried,
> Though that hir soules goon a-blakeberied.   (lines 119–20)

Here is a portrait of true corruption. The Pardoner is not excused by the fact that he was part of a corrupt system. Although he works solely for his own profit, the Church must have been fully aware of the dishonest methods of licensed pardoners, and condoned such practices where it enriched the Church. Chaucer's satirical portrait of a corrupt institution is focused through this single character.

The Pardoner's attempt to dupe the pilgrims

At the very end of his tale, with the story of the rioters concluded but fresh in mind, the Pardoner makes a sudden attempt to get the pilgrims to buy his services. Again, it is worth exploring alternative interpretations of this passage. One reading is that the Pardoner is so conceited that he reckons he can pull off the ultimate confidence trick, by revealing his trade secrets and then still brazenly demanding that the pilgrims take the bait. Such a view would mean that the Pardoner holds the pilgrims in complete contempt. When he provokingly suggests that the Host should begin because 'he is moost envoluped in sinne' (line 656), he picks on the least intellectually astute of the pilgrims. He perhaps hopes that the other pilgrims will laugh at the Host — but if the Host comes forward and buys a pardon, others are likely to follow suit. In this reading, the Host's rebuke comes as a horrid shock to the Pardoner, suggesting that the Host is not as stupid as he seems, or that the Pardoner is not as capable as he believes.

An alternative explanation is that the Pardoner truly believes that he can deceive the pilgrims, that he is so monstrously obsessed by his own skills that he thinks the pilgrims will fail to spot the significance of his confession. The Pardoner is driven by pride, the chief of the seven deadly sins, and this sin leads to a false sense of personal worth and capabilities (the rioters are similarly guilty). This reading may also take into account the fact that the Pardoner has insisted on drinking before he starts his tale (lines 41–42 and 170–72), and so overestimates his powers and maybe fails to notice how much he has given away. The rude awakening is much the same in this case, for the Host's retort proves that the Pardoner is deluded in a way that the Pardoner cannot mistake.

The Pardoner's own soul

This is a curious aspect of the tale. A more modern Pardoner might adopt an agnostic or atheistic position about the nature of the soul, of Heaven and Hell. He might consciously or unconsciously reject the notion of eternal damnation, and thus justify his own procedures to himself. But this can hardly be true in the Middle Ages. True atheism, and even agnosticism, were not available philosophical positions. God existed, Heaven and Hell existed; the fate of one's immortal soul depended on what a person did in his or her lifetime. What Chaucer presents is a godless man — a man so far turned from God that he no longer cares about the eternal consequences of his actions. He is a true criminal — a man who understands the evil of what he is doing, who knows the consequences, and yet who continues to do the thing anyway. This is not an uncommon phenomenon in everyday life; but it is exemplary to see how Chaucer presents a character who follows this course to its logical end. He functions as a pardoner, dealing in salvation and the amelioration of sin, yet he will not turn away from sin himself.

The Pardoner can be compared to Satan, who as Lucifer was an angel in Heaven, but who chose to defy God and was cast down into Hell. The Pardoner has a position of trust, and could work for the good of others, but he prefers to defy God and serve only himself. His reward, like Satan's, will be eternal damnation.

The Pardoner as a psychological case study

A modern reader is at liberty to construct psychological theories about the Pardoner. He can be seen as deluded or deranged; he may be considered to have an inadequate or damaged personality that seeks self-expression through the most provocative and outrageous behaviour. He always has to compete, and he always has to win — which is why his failure at the very end is so devastating for him. His uncertain sexuality, with a possible homoerotic relationship with the Summoner, offers further ground for consideration and discussion from a modern psychoanalytic perspective. All such theories can accommodate and make sense of his final challenge to the pilgrims, and his chagrin at being repulsed is certainly very naturalistic:

> So wrooth he was, no word ne wolde he seye.   (line 671)

The Pardoner's sexuality

Chaucer calls into the question the Pardoner's sexuality right back in 'The General Prologue':

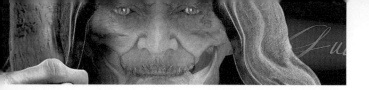

'I trowe he were a gelding or a mare.' (line 693)

This uncompromising statement is clearly meant to have symbolic significance, but the full force of it is not necessarily straightforward for a modern reader to recover.

In a simple sense, Chaucer may be providing a **metaphor** for the Pardoner's spiritual sterility. He is spiritually barren, dead to the Word of God and the awful implications of what he is doing. He confesses to mortal sin, but takes no steps to redeem himself. He subverts his sacred function by selling false pardons and offering false relics. He is even happy for others to go to Hell, provided he makes his profit.

A second significance of his sterility might be in relation to medieval notions of manhood. He is part of a patriarchal society, where men rule and women are subservient. The suggestion of his effeminacy ('a mare') would put him beneath all other men, unfit to play his proper role in society. The possibility of a homosexual relationship with the Summoner, with whom he sings love songs, would have been even more abhorrent. Homosexuality was seen as a vile sin by the Catholic Church, an attitude persisting to our own times in some quarters.

This lack of manhood might, where a psychological reading of the Pardoner is taken, partly account for his behaviour. The pilgrimage is full of strong, apparently successful men — the Knight, the Monk, the Host. Inadequate himself, the Pardoner gains his revenge on society and the hierarchy of his times by abusing his position and laughing at all those whom he fools:

'He made the person and the peple his apes.' ('The General Prologue', line 708)

His choice of the Host as a target at the end of his tale is consonant with this view. If he can get the better of a virile and dominant man, he can prove his own worth. As it is, he is horribly rebuffed.

The Pardoner as a literary construct

Equally, the Pardoner may be understood as a purely literary construct, with no 'personality' or psychology in a modern sense. This would state that Chaucer has constructed the figure purely in order to exemplify a characteristic, for example the sin of pride, and that he has no more reality than the allegorical characters in the medieval morality plays or in Bunyan's *The Pilgrim's Progress*. In this case every aspect of his prologue and tale are exemplifications of a character type, and the ending of his tale is not meant to seem naturalistic or probable — that is not its function. Its purpose is to show how deeply self-deluding a sinful soul can be.

There is no conflict between this interpretation and the portrayal of the Pardoner in realistic terms. Items like the husband's sudden blindness in 'The Merchant's Tale' or the behaviour of 'patient Griselda' in 'The Clerk's Tale' are adequate proof that Chaucer was able to combine a high degree of realism with entirely symbolic events.

Aspects of language

The Pardoner's use of language

The Pardoner is a professional speaker — he is used to preaching, and knows how to engage an audience. Apart from the Parson, he is the most accomplished public speaker amongst the pilgrims.

Chaucer makes him eloquent, but varies his speech from the formal and rhetorical nature of his preaching to the casual conversational style he uses with the other pilgrims. It is this blending of the formal and the informal that gives the character of the Pardoner such complexity and apparent realism.

Every line offers potential examples for discussion, so the following are offered only as starting points.

Conversational and colloquial elements of the Pardoner's speech

Conversational style

This is most evident at those moments when he is speaking to the other pilgrims, at the end of the introduction and at the end of his prologue.

> I graunte, ywis,' quod he, 'but I moot thinke
> Upon some honest thing while that I drinke.   (lines 41–42)

> But herkneth, lordinges, in conclusioun:
> Youre liking is that I shal telle a tale.   (lines 168–69)

Colloquial words and phrases

It shal be doon.	(line 34)
alle and some	(line 50)
a-blakeberied	(line 120)
Now hoold youre pees!	(line 176)
a stiked swyn	(line 270)

Conversational sentence structures

> Allas, a foul thing is it, by my feith,
> To seye this word, and fouler is the dede   (lines 238–39)

> But herkneth, lordinges, o word, I yow preye.   (line 287)

Formal elements in the Pardoner's use of language

Rhetoric

The Pardoner, as a professional speaker, makes much use of the rhetorical techniques that were an intrinsic part of medieval education, and which were developed systematically in the Middle Ages by writers such as Geoffrey of Vinsauf.

Rhetoric was one of the seven liberal arts taught in universities. It is not necessary for A-level students to be familiar with the classical terms such as *occupatio*, *amplificatio* and *abbreviatio*, but they should be able to recognise features. There is an excellent website, aptly named 'The Forest of Rhetoric', at http://humanities. byu.edu/rhetoric/silva.htm, which will assist students who wish to explore further.

Rhetorical questions are instantly visible:

What nedeth it to sermone of it moore? (line 593)

The whole of his tale involves *amplificatio*, the gradual accretion of material to add emphasis and force to an idea.

Most striking of all is the Pardoner's frequent use of **exclamatio**, or more precisely *ecphonesis*, that is to say emotional exclamation. It features in lines 212–14, line 248, line 265, but these are all in a way preparatory to the grand finale to his story in lines 609–11.

Exempla

The most noticeably formal and rhetorical aspect of 'The Pardoner's Tale' is the way he uses lists of examples to support his case. This may seem unusual to modern eyes, but was commonplace in medieval literature, where authorities counted for so much. Having begun his story about the 'compaignye/Of yonge folk' (lines 177–78), the Pardoner interposes a series of *exempla* to develop his theme. This occupies lines 197–373. The Bible is his main source, but he ranges freely across Classical and later authorities, from Seneca to John of Salisbury.

Formal vocabulary

It is obvious that the Pardoner will use technical terms associated with his vocation — 'theme' (line 47), 'patente' (line 51), 'predicacioun' (line 59), 'ensamples' (line 149). He also uses formal vocabulary to make himself sound superior — for example 'hauteyn' (line 44), 'pronounce' (line 49), 'saffron' (line 59). He also claims he uses Latin (line 58), particularly in stating his theme (line 48).

Formal sentence structures

His use of formal sentence structures is evident throughout his prologue and tale, never more so than in the story-telling 'once upon a time' opening of his tale:

In Flaundres whilom was a compaignye
Of yonge folk that haunteden folye. (lines 177–78)

The Pardoner's voice

It can be disputed whether Chaucer gives the Pardoner an individual voice. The Pardoner is not as immediately distinctive as the Wife of Bath, for example, whose free-flowing and garrulous utterance is brilliantly depicted by Chaucer. Much of his speech is conscious and formal, both in his prologue and his tale. At the same time,

the depth and brazenness of his self-confession resonates and remains highly memorable:

> Thus spitte I out my venym under hewe
> Of hoolinesse, to semen hooly and trewe.　　　　　　　　(lines 135–36)

This seems to catch an individual voice — the image of the Pardoner 'spitting' poison like a snake; the repetition of 'holy' in the second line to emphasise the deceit that he uses. The Pardoner may eventually be a literary figure composed in a non-naturalistic age, but he comes across to the modern reader as a fully-realised character. The combination of homely image and God-defying arrogance in lines 119–20 are sharply effective in giving the impression of a true individual:

> I rekke nevere, whan that they been beried,
> Though that hir soules goon a-blakeberied.

Blasphemy

It is difficult for a modern reader to understand the importance of blasphemy as an aspect of 'The Pardoner's Prologue and Tale'. An expression like 'God's teeth' may seem frankly mild or inconsequential, and casual swearing is commonplace nowadays. Although the crime of blasphemy was only finally abolished in English law in 2008, it had been diminished to the status of common law since the seventeenth century.

Yet in the Middle Ages, blasphemy was one of the most appalling of all crimes. It was abhorrent because it entailed disrespect or disregard for God. Blasphemy means having an impious (literally *im-pious*, not pious and respectful) attitude to God, leading to irreverent utterances or actions. The importance of piety goes right back to God's commandment: 'Thou shalt not take the name of the Lord thy God in vain.'

It is in this context that blasphemy in *The Canterbury Tales* needs to be understood. Equally, it is necessary to distinguish even here between a casual utterance that even a normally respectful person might lapse into, and the kind of hardened impiety that is on display in 'The Pardoner's Prologue and Tale'.

The Host, for example, swears in the Introduction, 'by nailes and by blood!' (line 2), a reference to the nails with which Christ was crucified and the blood spilt in doing so. In a strict sense this is clearly blasphemy, and the Pardoner is right to describe the Host as being 'envoluped in sinne' (line 656). Chaucer makes no attempt to assert that the Host is a particularly moral or virtuous man, and in this he is merely being realistic. Clearly people swore in the Middle Ages as they do nowadays. But the Host is just an innkeeper, not a servant of the Church, there is no malice in him, and his oaths are casual, more a mannerism than a sign of ingrained irreverence. Chaucer intends us to understand that there are degrees of behaviour; the Host is a mild sinner, but the rioters and the Pardoner are in a different category altogether.

It is worth comparing how the Pardoner describes the swearing of the revellers at the start of his tale:

> Hir othes been so grete and so dampnable
> That it is grisly for to heere hem swere.
> Oure blissed Lordes body they totere —
> Hem thoughte that Jewes rente him noght ynough   (lines 186–89)

The Pardoner equates swearing with the literal tearing of Christ's body, comparable to his Crucifixion. This seems extreme to modern eyes, but it reflects the common medieval view of the nature of blasphemy. He later develops this point further:

> Lo, rather he forbedeth swich swering
> Than homicide or many a cursed thing   (lines 357–58)

This is even more stark. Blasphemy is worse than homicide because it is God who is being 'killed' by such oaths.

The rioters as blasphemers

It is in the characters of the three rioters that the Pardoner, and Chaucer, embody the sins that make it clear how appalling blasphemy is.

The rioters swear freely, both to each other and to the old man — for example, in lines 406, 415, 464, 466, 471. These are gratuitous blasphemous utterances, and the Pardoner confirms the depths of their depravity:

> And many a grisly ooth thanne han they sworn,
> And Cristes blessed body al torente   (lines 422–23)

The Pardoner ensures that all aspects of their behaviour are sinful, and thereby blasphemous. They are drunk before dawn (lines 375–77), they swear false oaths of loyalty and brotherhood (lines 416–17), they abuse the old man as soon as they meet him (lines 430–33), they are consumed with greed (lines 486–89) and they conspire against and kill each other (lines 594–602). At no point do they manifest any pious Christian attitudes or behaviour.

The Pardoner as a blasphemer

The depth of Chaucer's art is clear from the way that he makes the Pardoner, who presents such a stark portrayal of blasphemy through the rioters, as guilty as they are. True, the Pardoner deliberately avoids verbal blasphemy in both his prologue and his tale. Clearly he is conscious of his position and knows that too many oaths will alienate his audience. He swears only when he is off guard, speaking to the pilgrims at the inn before he tells his tale. He picks up the Host's oath 'by Seint Ronyon!' (line 34), and adds his own 'By God' (line 171). The fact that he swears at all is inappropriate, given his vocation.

However, it is in his behaviour that the Pardoner is utterly impious. Like the rioters, he wants to start off by being gluttonous (lines 35–36) when he should be reflecting in a devout manner about what he is going to say. He is careless about others' salvation (lines 117–20), and even about his own (lines 141–42). He freely admits the fraudulence of his relics (line 63), and worst of all he usurps the power of a priest by claiming to have the power to absolve people of their sins (line 627). His flagrant attempt to dupe the Host shows his contempt both for other people and for the God whom he is supposed to serve. He is guilty of hubris — inviting God's wrath by ignoring the consequences of his own actions. This disdain towards God and total impiety represents blasphemy of the highest order.

Humour

Chaucer is a richly comic poet, and much of *The Canterbury Tales* is meant to be entertaining, even where it contains serious moral points as well. His use of irony is dealt with below, but he uses other techniques as well.

Parody

The Pardoner's story of the three rioters can be seen as a parody of a conventional medieval knightly quest:

The questers. Traditionally, quests were undertaken by knights, who were of noble birth, chivalrous, Christian and devout. In the Pardoner's story the rioters are commoners, with no courtesy (consider their treatment of the old man), and un-Christian (consider the oaths they continually swear). They are dissolute gamblers and drunkards.

The quest. Conventionally, a quest would be to do a good deed, for example to slay a malicious monster that threatens ordinary people. The Pardoner's story is of a quest to slay Death itself, which is an absurdity. The tale gains its force because it is a subversion of all that is noble or honourable, and a parody of the kind of conventional knightly story such as that told by Chaucer's own Knight at the start of *The Canterbury Tales*.

The outcome. Conventionally, the noble knight succeeds in his quest and gains honour and fortune from doing so. The rioters ironically achieve their quest too, but this inevitably means their own deserved deaths. The audience feels no sympathy for them because of their evil natures.

Situational and verbal humour

'The Pardoner's Prologue and Tale' is full of comic effects. A few examples are given below:

> 'I graunte, ywis,' quod he, 'but I moot thinke
> Upon som honest thing while that I drinke.'   (lines 41–42)

The humour here lies in the tension between the words 'honest' and 'drinke', which do not naturally sit together — unless the audience subscribes to the idea of *in vino veritas*, and believe that the Pardoner's open confession of his tricks takes place because he is drunk. The Pardoner's story, however, is too well controlled for us to believe that this is the case. Chaucer does not say so, but some commentators have considered it likely that the Pardoner recounts the whole of his tale while sitting outside an inn. This would be particularly appropriate, given that much of his speech is about the perils of drunkenness.

> Ther cam a privee theef men clepeth Deeth,
> That in this contree al the peple sleeth　　　　　　　　　　(lines 389–90)

This is beautifully worded by Chaucer. It is necessarily true that all people are slain by Death. The inn servant's personification is glibly accepted by the rioters.

> And preyde him that he him wolde selle
> Som poison, that he mighte his rattes quelle.　　　　　　　(lines 567–68)

These lines suggest that the two elder rioters are rats — very apt considering their treacherous behaviour.

> Deeth shal be deed, if that they may him hente.　　　　　　(line 424)

The humour here lies in the beautifully controlled contrast between the rash arrogance of the rioters — 'Deeth shal be deed' — and the deflating word 'if' that follows. 'If' they could capture Death they might slay him — but in fact Death will capture them.

Bawdiness

Chaucer is famous for the **bawdy** aspects of some of his tales, and is sometimes presented as if he were primarily a writer of bawdy comedy. In reality, such tales are in a minority in *The Canterbury Tales*, but are more immediately appealing to modern audiences than the stern moralising of 'The Tale of Melibee' and 'The Parson's Tale'. In 'The Pardoner's Tale', bawdy language is restricted to a single passage, which gives its coarseness greater force:

> 'I wolde I hadde thy coillons in myn hond
> In stide of relikes or of seintuarie.
> Lat kutte hem of, I wol thee helpe hem carie;
> They shul be shrined in an hogges toord!'　　　　　　　　(lines 666–69)

These lines are richly comic because of their crudity, but they are thematic too. The Host condemns the Pardoner's false relics, and all false relics, by suggesting that the Pardoner's testicles would be worth just as much. Moreover, there is a clear reference back to line 693 of 'The General Prologue':

I trowe he were a gelding or a mare.

That comment was from Chaucer the Pilgrim, and this indicates that the Pardoner's sexuality was a source of rude jokes for all the pilgrims. The suggestion there that he may already have been castrated raises the subtle implication that he may previously have fallen foul of a man like the Host, and perhaps for similar reasons. This can hardly be the first time that he has boasted about his skills as a pardoner. The Host's remark in this case becomes doubly cutting if the Pardoner has no testicles to lose.

Irony

Much of *The Canterbury Tales* is humorous, and Chaucer uses many types of comedy. However, 'The Pardoner's Prologue and Tale' is dominated by the use of irony. If you have studied 'The General Prologue' you should be well aware of the varieties of irony that Chaucer uses, some subtle and some blatant.

The complexity in 'The Pardoner's Prologue and Tale' is that while Chaucer uses irony to expose the corruption of the Pardoner, the Pardoner also uses it himself.

The Pardoner's use of irony

The Pardoner is deeply aware of the irony of his own vocation:

> Thus kan I preche again that same vice
> Which that I use, and that is avarice.   (lines 141–42)

Hence his deliberate selection of his only preaching theme:

> *Radix malorum est Cupiditas.* ('The love of money is the root of all evil.')
>   (line 48)

He seems to take delight in preaching very precisely about the sin of avarice, when he knows that it is his own motivating force. Similarly, he revels in the irony of his own ability to make others genuinely repent, while he remains a confirmed sinner:

> But though myself be gilty in that sinne,
> Yet kan I maken oother folk to twynne
> From avarice, and soore to repente.   (lines 143–45)

Additionally, he makes active use of irony in his preaching, when he condemns sinners amongst his congregation:

> Swich folk shal have no power ne no grace
> To offren to my relikes in this place.   (lines 97–98)

He knows the irony of his message — if the relics have no effect, it is because the person seeking their aid has unconfessed sins that invalidate the offering. No insurance salesman could more neatly trap his customers in a web of words.

In the story he tells of the three rioters, the Pardoner makes active use of irony to make his points more striking and memorable. It is the wilful blindness of the rioters that is most harshly highlighted, as when they speak of seeking Death:

> 'Is it swich peril with him for to meete?'   (line 407)

or when they find the gold:

> No lenger thanne after Deeth they soughte.   (line 486)

The fact that the money is death leads to further ironies of which the rioters are unaware:

> This tresor hath Fortune unto us yiven.   (line 493)

This idea is repeated four lines later when the speaker refers to the coins/death as 'so fair a grace' (line 497).

The depth of the rioters' self-deception is clear when they talk of removing the money by night in case they are seen:

> Men wolde seyn that we were theves stronge,
> And for oure owene tresor doon us honge.   (lines 503–04)

A more subtle usage is when the rioter accuses the old man of being in league with Death:

> For soothly thou art oon of his assent
> To sleen us yonge folk, thou false theef!   (lines 472–73)

There has been no suggestion of such an alliance, but the old man promptly obliges by showing them the way to death if they are determined.

The Pardoner's employment of irony is deepened by his willingness in turn to assign it to the old man, whose more mild use of it yet retains all its force. This starts when he replies to their abusive challenge about his age by gently claiming that nobody 'wolde chaunge his youthe for myn age' (line 438). By the time they leave him they have driven him to a more open use of irony, which they still refuse to understand:

> 'Now, sires,' quod he, 'if that yow be so leef
> To finde Deeth, turne up this croked wey'   (lines 474–75)

He is well aware that the word Death is being used metaphorically, even if they aren't.

Outside the story of the rioters, the Pardoner's irony once again reflects on his own behaviour:

> Now, goode men, God foryeve yow youre trespas,
> And ware yow fro the sinne of avarice!
> Myn hooly pardoun may yow alle warice,
> So that ye offre nobles or sterlinges'   (lines 618–21)

The only time his control of irony breaks down is at the very end. He hopes to ironically persuade the pilgrims to buy his wares even after he has confessed their falsehood. The Host's ability to see straight through the irony and trickery is a major blow to the Pardoner's self-esteem and beliefs.

Chaucer's use of irony against the Pardoner

The ironies to which the Pardoner himself is subject to are seen also to be direct comments from Chaucer:

> *Radix malorum est Cupiditas.*   (line 48)

That, if we like, is Chaucer's own theme in his entire portrayal of the Pardoner. He is exposing the corruption and evil caused by a man's obsession with personal gain, the corruption that has caused this loathsome man to subvert the functions of the Church and to sacrifice his immortal soul for the sake of short-term worldly wealth. His very profession is profoundly ironic — the man most in need of Christ's pardon is the Pardoner himself, but he does not seek it.

The corruption of pardoners was widely recognised in the fourteenth century, and Chaucer's educated audience would have been alert for signs that this one is wicked. Chaucer's portrayal can therefore be an uncompromising attack on the character and the way he preys on less sophisticated people.

There is savage irony when he has the Pardoner say:

> That no man be so boold, ne preest ne clerk,
> Me to destourbe of Cristes hooly werk.   (lines 53–54)

It is not 'Cristes hooly werk', and doubtless any true priest or cleric would wish to stop him offering false hopes and false salvation.

The Pardoner's expertise is a source of dismay for Chaucer:

> Mine handes and my tonge goon so yerne
> That it is joye to se my bisynesse.   (lines 112–13)

It is despicable to see such talents used to such false ends. We need to remember that the Pardoner is careless of others' souls provided that he makes monetary gain.

Every time that the Pardoner condemns sin, the audience is aware that he condemns himself:

> But certes, he that haunteth swiche delices
> Is deed, whil that he liveth in tho vices.   (lines 261–62)

In addition to his avarice, the audience has not forgotten that the Pardoner refuses to tell a story without a drink first (lines 35–36).

The tale of the rioters, of course, gains its extra level of resonance, as if it needed one, from the fact that their obsession with gold mirrors the Pardoner's own.

Finally, Chaucer's greatest use of irony is reserved for the end of the tale. The Pardoner, the master manipulator and employer of irony, is brought crashing to earth through the greatest irony of all, his complete miscalculation about the Host's perspicacity. The simplicity and directness of the description of the Pardoner's discomfiture:

> This Pardoner answerde nat a word.   (line 670)

provides the culmination of all the ironies present throughout 'The Pardoner's Prologue and Tale'.

It is worth considering that Chaucer's condemnation of the Pardoner also highlights the corruption of the medieval church, which licensed or condoned pardoners.

Critical approaches

All literary texts are subject to revaluation with the passage of time, and critical approaches will vary according to the concerns and preoccupations that apply in the critic's period. Each student, quite properly, evaluates the text for themselves. Your own considered opinion is what matters, but it should be based on the most detailed and measured analysis of which you are capable. 'The Pardoner's Prologue and Tale' is a fertile ground for varied critical approaches, because there is so much controversy about the nature of the Pardoner himself. As a result, it is possible to identify a range of critical stances that have been taken over time. It is up to you to decide the worth of each. Each of the approaches below should be considered and its validity discussed.

(1) Historical criticism and New Historicism

Historical critics tend to look at *The Canterbury Tales* as entirely a product of its time, and look at it entirely within its original context. Some early critics even tried to find real-life counterparts of Chaucer's pilgrims, whereas other looked at Chaucer in terms of medieval literary schemes such as allegory, or the representation of what was called Estates Satire, examining the nature of society at the time. New Historicists look further afield to the whole cultural background of texts, attempting to see how texts were formed by and reflected the historical, political, religious, economic and social circumstances within which they were written. In the case of the Pardoner, a great deal of attention has been paid to the role of pardoners in the

medieval Church, and how far Chaucer's portrayal is based on genuine contemporary practice.

(2) Psychoanalytic criticism

The apparent roundness of the Pardoner's character makes him an obvious candidate for psychoanalytical **criticism**, which attempts to subject literary characters to the same kind of forensic analysis as would be applied to real human beings. It is easy to dismiss this approach, as a literary construct manifestly is exactly that — an artificial construct produced by an author for a particular purpose. In the Middle Ages this was certainly true — characters were often severely limited in scope, perhaps metaphorically or allegorically representing a single characteristic or idea. However, a psychoanalytical approach can promote valuable insights if caution is exercised, and this is especially true of the Pardoner. His confession and his exposure of his methods require explanation, and an approach that concentrates on his possible state of mind seems quite natural to a twenty-first-century reader. The Pardoner can be seen as deluded, or as compensating for his sexual inadequacy by boasting of his other powers. He could even be seen as mildly schizophrenic, when he tries to make the pilgrims buy his wares at the end, as if he is unaware that he has previously confessed to being a fraud. A psychoanalytical approach offers a very modern way of looking at a very medieval work, and discretion should be exercised in evaluating its worth.

(3) Marxist criticism

Marxist critics look for what literary texts have to say about the power relations between various classes or economic groups within society. Chaucer's work is a rich source of material because it appears to be written at a time when many of the traditional models of interrelationship, particularly the concepts embodied in feudalism, were breaking down, and society was metamorphosing into something more recognisably modern. The Church too was constantly threatened by internal feuding, which would lead a century later to the Reformation. Marxist political philosophy sees established religion as essentially repressive, and this would clearly be true in the case of the medieval Church. The Pardoner in one sense represents this oppression, playing on people's fears to extort money from them. However, the Pardoner is himself exploiting the power of the Church, because he uses its cover for his personal gain. In this way he can be seen to be manipulating the power relationship between the individual and the Church in his own interest, and might be viewed less harshly in this light than when considered solely as a moral agent.

(4) Dramatic theory

This approach to literature entails looking at the text within its context, in this case *The Canterbury Tales*, and examining the way that the parts are built up to form a

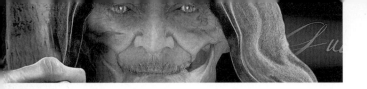

dramatic whole. In the case of 'The Pardoner's Prologue and Tale' this approach can be used in two ways. It is possible to look at the Pardoner in relation to the other pilgrims, and his tale in relation to other tales. There is clearly a 'dramatic' tension between him and the Wife of Bath for example. They are the two characters given extended prologues by Chaucer, and her extreme sexuality is contrasted by his lack of it. He interrupts the Wife's prologue, and receives a sharp rebuke from her.

Equally, it is possible to examine the dramatic elements with 'The Pardoner's Prologue and Tale' — there are a range of voices at work, from the Pardoner and the Host to the characters within the tale, each offering a different perspective on the nature of experience and ways of living. The use of **dialogue** and setting is also comparable to theatre. There is an arching dramatic form reaching from the inter-action of the Pardoner and the Host in the Introduction to their final explosive confrontation at the end of 'The Pardoner's Tale'.

(5) Deconstructionist criticism

This is probably the most difficult type of literary theory for the student to grasp easily because it challenges the idea that texts can offer 'true' meanings. The nature of language itself means that words can never say exactly what we intend them to mean. Deconstructionists frequently look at the gaps and ambiguities in the language of a text. For this reason every reading of a text can be challenged by a counter-reading, and meaning remains elusive or undefinable. In the case of the Pardoner this can lead to the stripping away of notions of character and characterisation to examine the uncertainties and ambiguities contained in the language Chaucer uses.

(6) Feminist criticism

Feminist criticism, one of the more prominent of modern critical approaches, has little to say about the 'The Pardoner's Prologue and Tale' because it contains no female characters. The Church was hostile to women, the Pardoner inhabits a world dominated exclusively by men, and he is evidently a misogynist, as demonstrated by his interruption in 'The Wife of Bath's Prologue'. The rioters, the old man, the innkeeper and servant are all male. Ironically, it is the Pardoner himself whose sexuality is ambivalent, with the suggestions that he is either homosexual or a eunuch.

Useful quotations

The best quotations are those you have found useful in class discussions and practice essays, and they will require little conscious learning because you are already familiar with them. The most effective ones to learn in addition are those that serve more than one purpose, i.e. those that can be used to support a theme, image, or style usage, as well as a point about character or narrative effect.

'I graunte, ywis,' quod he, 'but I moot thinke
Upon some honest thing while that I drinke.'   (lines 41–42)
There is an immediate ironic tension between the words 'honeste' and 'drinke'.

I peyne me to han an hauteyn speche.   (line 44)
This shows both the Pardoner's skill and his pride.

Radix malorum est Cupiditas.   (line 48)
*Latin for 'money is at the root of all evil', this is the central theme of 'The
Pardoner's Prologue and Tale', as well as of the Pardoner's sermons.*

Relikes been they, as wenen they echoon.   (line 63)
The Pardoner confesses the falseness of his relics.

So that he offre pens, or elles grotes.   (line 90)
The Pardoner's avarice is always visible.

Swich folk shal have no power ne no grace
To offren to my relikes in this place.   (lines 97–98)
This is the Pardoner's clever let-out clause to prevent recriminations.

Mine handes and my tonge goon so yerne
That it is joye to se my bisynesse.   (lines 112–13)
Again, the Pardoner delights in his own skill.

For myn entente is nat but for to winne,
And nothing for correccioun of sinne.
I rekke nevere, whan that they been beried,
Though that hir soules goon a-blakeberied.   (lines 117–20)
*The central and most damning confession of the Pardoner's unscrupulous and
immoral character.*

Thus spitte I out my venym under hewe
Of hoolinesse, to semen hooly and trewe.   (lines 135–36)
The Pardoner's spitefulness is aptly caught in the image of a snake.

Thus kan I preche again that same vice
Which that I use, and that is avarice.   (lines 141–42)
The Pardoner's self-awareness can be seen as admirable, or horrifying.

But though myself be gilty in that sinne,
Yet kan I maken oother folk to twynne
From avarice, and soore to repente.   (lines 143–45)
The Pardoner notes the ironic positive effect that his sermons can have.

I will have money, wool, cheese and wheat

I wol have moneie, wolle, chese, and whete,
Al were it yeven of the povereste page,
Or of the povereste widwe in a village   (lines 162–65)
Another chilling confession of the Pardoner's nature.

But herkneth, lordinges, in conclusioun:
Youre liking is that I shal telle a tale.   (lines 168–69)
The Pardoner knows the pilgrims wish to be entertained.

For though myself be a ful vicious man,
A moral tale yet I yow telle kan   (lines 173–74)
Another example of the Pardoner's self-awareness.

They daunce and pleyen at dees bothe day and night,
And eten also and drinken over hir might   (lines 181–82)
The revellers are guilty of many sins.

Hir othes been so grete and so dampnable
That it is grisly for to heere hem swere.
Oure blissed Lordes body they totere —
Hem thoughte that Jewes rente him noght ynough   (lines 186–89)
Blasphemy is the most evil of their crimes.

And ech of hem at otheres sinne lough.   (line 190)
The revellers are unrepentant.

But certes, he that haunteth swiche delices
Is deed, whil that he liveth in tho vices.   (lines 261–62)
The Pardoner condemns the revellers — and himself — unequivocally.

For dronkenesse is verray sepulture
Of mannes wit and his discrecioun.   (lines 272–73)
The modern reader might recognise the truth of this as surely as Chaucer's audience
would have done.

Lo, rather he forbedeth swich swering
Than homicide or many a cursed thing   (lines 357–58)
The Pardoner makes an important claim about the relative nature of sins.

This fruit cometh of the bicched bones two,
Forswering, ire, falsnesse, homicide.   (lines 371–72)
This may seem extreme to the modern reader, but the Pardoner is linking all the
sins together.

Thise riotoures thre of whiche I telle (line 375)

The Pardoner has not, of course, identified three particular individuals previously.
This is a rhetorical trick to engage the audience instantly in the narrative.

'Ther cam a privee theef men clepeth Deeth,
That in this contree al the peple sleeth. (line 389–90)

The personification of Death is macabre, and forms the basis for what follows.

Ye, Goddes armes! (line 406)

The rioter commits blasphemy.

Is it swich peril with him for to meete? (line 407)

One of Chaucer's wonderful comic ironies. It is surely perilous to meet one's death.

He shal be slain, he that so manye sleeth,
By Goddes dignitee, er it be night. (lines 414–15)

The rioter's boast is grotesque, and comically empty. Swearing the oath in God's
name makes it worse.

And many a grisly ooth thanne han they sworn,
And Cristes blessed body al torente. (lines 422–23)

Again, the Pardoner emphasises the rioters' blasphemy.

Deeth shal be deed, if that they may him hente. (line 424)

Death, of course, will take them instead.

Why livestow so longe in so greet age? (line 433)

The rioter is abusive to the old man.

For I ne kan nat finde / A man...
That wolde chaunge his youthe for myn age (lines 435–36, 438)

The old man is wryly mild in response.

And on the ground, which is my moodres gate,
I knokke with my staf, bothe erly and late,
And seye, "Leeve mooder, leet me in!" (lines 443–45)

A compelling image of the old man knocking 'at death's door'.

Lo how I vanisshe, flessh and blood and skin!
Allas! whan shul my bones been at reste? (lines 446–47)

A classic medieval image of mortality.

'Now, sires,' quod he, 'if that yow be so leef
To finde Deeth, turne up this croked wey,
For in that grove I lafte him, by my fey' (lines 474–76)

The centre of the tale. The image of 'the croked wey' is resonant.

No lenger thanne after Deeth they soughte (line 486)
Another of Chaucer's comic ironies. They have found Death.

This tresor hath Fortune unto us yiven,
In mirthe and joliftee oure lyf to liven. (lines 493–94)
The rioters' self-delusion prevents pity for their fate.

For-why the feend foond him in swich livinge
That he hadde leve him to sorwe bringe. (lines 561–62)
The Pardoner emphasises the evil lifestyle of the rioters.

What nedeth it to sermone of it moore? (line 593)
The Pardoner brings his tale to an abrupt conclusion.

O cursed sinne of alle cursednesse!
O traitours homicide, O wikkednesse! (lines 609–10)
The Pardoner's powerful exclamation at the end of his tale.

Myn hooly pardoun may yow alle warice,
So that ye offre nobles or sterlinges (lines 620–21)
The Pardoner falsely usurps the power of a priest to offer absolution.

I yow assoille by myn heigh power. (line 627)
He claims directly to be able to offer absolution for sins.

Paraventure ther may fallen oon or two
Doun of his hors, and breke his nekke atwo. (lines 649–50)
The Pardoner gives a macabre reminder of the frail nature of human existence.

'I wolde I hadde thy coillons in myn hond
In stide of relikes or of seintuarie.
Lat kutte hem of, I wol thee helpe hem carie;
They shul be shrined in an hogges toord!' (lines 666–69)
The Host's thundering rejoinder is the comic climax of 'The Pardoner's Tale'.

This Pardoner answerde nat a word;
So wrooth he was, no word ne wolde he seye. (lines 670–71)
Ironically, the eloquent Pardoner is silenced.

Literary terms and concepts

Assessment Objective 1 requires 'informed and relevant responses to literary texts, using appropriate terminology and concepts'. A knowledge of literary terms is therefore essential for A-level literature students, and allows responses to texts to

CITY AND ISLINGTON
SIXTH FORM COLLEGE
283 - 309 GOSWELL ROAD
LONDON

be worded precisely and concisely. The terms and concepts below have been selected for their relevance to the study of *The Canterbury Tales*.

abbreviatio (rhetoric):	the opposite of *amplificatio*. The shortening of an idea or statement to make an emphatic point, e.g. 'Right so they han him slain' ('The Pardoner's Tale', line 595).
allegory:	extended metaphor which veils a moral, religious or political underlying meaning
alliteration:	repetition of initial letter or sound in adjacent words to create an atmospheric or onomatopoeic effect, e.g. 'straunge strondes' ('The General Prologue', line 13)
ambiguity:	capacity of words to have two meanings in the context as a device for enriching meaning
amplificatio (rhetoric):	extending ideas or statements in order to build a rhetorical effect
analogue:	a text which bears a marked similarity to another
analogy:	perception of similarity between two things
apostrophise:	directly address a divinity, object or abstract concept, such as gluttony ('The Pardoner's Tale', line 226)
archetype:	original model used as recurrent symbol, e.g. the brave knight
bathos:	sudden change of register from the sublime to the ridiculous
bawdy:	lewd; with coarse, humorous references to sex
characterisation:	means by which fictional characters are personified and made distinctive
circumlocutio (rhetoric):	the replacement of a word or idea by a descriptive phrase
climax:	moment of intensity to which a series of events has been leading
colloquial:	informal language of conversational speech
contextuality:	historical, social and cultural background of a text
couplet:	two consecutive lines of poetry that are paired in rhyme
courtly love:	in the Middle Ages a code governing the behaviour of aristocratic lovers, with a subservient lover adoring an idealised woman
criticism:	evaluation of literary text or other artistic work
denouement:	unfolding of the final stages of a plot, when all is revealed
dialogue:	direct speech of characters engaged in conversation
didactic:	with the intention of teaching the reader and instilling moral values

ecphonesis (rhetoric):	an emotional exclamation, e.g. 'O wombe! O bely! O stinking cod...! ('The Pardoner's Tale', line 248)
elements:	earth, air, fire, water, of which it was believed in the Middle Ages that the universe was composed, with corresponding humours to explain human temperament
empathy:	identifying with a character in a literary work
end-stopped:	line of poetry which ends with some form of punctuation, creating a pause
enjamb(e)ment:	run-on instead of end-stopped line of poetry, usually to reflect meaning
exclamatio (rhetoric):	a rhetorical exclamation
fabliau:	short medieval tale in rhyme, of a coarsely comic and satirical nature
figurative:	using imagery; non-literal use of language
genre:	type or form of writing with identifiable characteristics, e.g. fairy tale, fabliau
heroic couplet:	iambic pentameter rhymed in pairs; traditional form of classical epic poetry
hubris:	arrogance or over-confidence, especially where this is likely to result in disaster
humours:	four bodily fluids produced by different organs and related to one of the elements, an excess of which caused particular temperaments: yellow bile (anger), blood (happiness), phlegm (calm), black bile (melancholy)
hyperbole:	deliberate exaggeration for effect, e.g. 'Ther was no man nowher so vertuous' ('The General Prologue', line 251)
iambic pentameter:	five feet of iambs, i.e. unstressed/stressed alternating syllables
imagery:	descriptive language appealing to the senses; imagery may be sustained or recurring throughout texts, usually in the form of simile or metaphor
irony:	a discrepancy between the actual and implied meaning of language; or an amusing or cruel reversal of an outcome expected, intended or deserved; situation in which one is mocked by fate or the facts
juxtaposition:	placing side by side for (ironic) contrast of interpretation
metaphor:	suppressed comparison implied not stated, e.g. when the Pardoner speaks of Christ as 'oure soules leche' ('The Pardoner's Tale, line 630)
metre:	regular series of stressed and unstressed syllables in a line of poetry

narrative:	connected and usually chronological series of events that form a story
parody:	imitation and exaggeration of style for purpose of humour and ridicule
personification:	a figure of speech in which an abstract idea is given human form or characteristics — notably Death in 'The Pardoner's Tale'
plot:	cause-and-effect sequence of events caused by characters' actions
register:	level of formality of expression
rhetoric:	art of persuasion using emotive language and stylistic devices, e.g. triple structures or rhetorical questions: 'What nedeth it to sermone of it moore?' ('The Pardoner's Tale', line 593)
rhyme:	repetition of final vowel sound in words at the end of lines of poetry
rhythm:	pace and sound pattern of writing, created by metre, vowel length, syntax and punctuation
romance:	story of love and heroism, deriving from medieval court life and fairy tale
satire:	exposing of vice or foolishness of a person or institution to ridicule
scansion:	system of notation for marking stressed (/) and unstressed (~) syllables in a line of metrical verse
seven deadly sins:	according to the medieval Catholic Church, the following sins were mortal and led straight to Hell: pride, envy, anger, sloth, avarice, gluttony, lust
simile:	comparison introduced by 'as' or 'like', e.g. the Monk's head 'that shoon as any glas' ('The General Prologue', line 198)
stereotype:	category of person with typical characteristics, often used for mockery
syntax:	arrangement of grammar and word order in sentence construction
theme:	abstract idea or issue explored in a text
tone:	emotional aspect of the voice of a text, e.g. Chaucer the author's ironic tone, when he says of the Friar, 'Unto his ordre he was a noble post' ('The General Prologue', line 214)
wit:	intelligent verbal humour

Questions & Answers

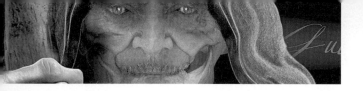

Essay questions, specimen plans and notes

OCR (closed text, 30 marks out of 60 in a 2-hour exam)

'The Pardoner's Prologue and Tale'

1 'Much literature explores the tension between what should be and what is, in a corrupt society.' By comparing one drama and one poetry text you have studied, explore ways in which this assertion seems to you to be relevant.

Issues to consider when making a plan
- how the authors in the chosen texts convey a sense of what 'should be'
- how the authors show corrupt behaviour within their characters
- the importance of contextual factors both in the production and reception of texts
- the personal response of the informed reader to these moral and social tensions
- the awareness of alternative responses
- the differing effects of poetic and dramatic genres

2 'Comic writing essentially stems from deception and disguise.' By comparing one drama and one poetry text you have studied, explore how far and in what ways you think this assertion is valid.

3 By comparing one drama and one poetry text you have studied, discuss ways in which writers explore the dangers and delights of ambition.

4 By comparing one drama and one poetry text you have studied, discuss ways in which writers explore the idea of a personal hell.

OCR marking guidance for Question 1 (Band 6: 26–30 marks)

AO1	consistently fluent, analytical writing
AO1	confident, perceptive evaluation of the tension between what should be and what is, in a corrupt society in well-structured, informed argument
AO2	consistently well-informed and perceptive discussion of effects (including dramatic effects) of language, form and structure
AO3	(well-developed), perceptive and sustained comparative analysis of relationships between texts
AO3	perceptive judgements consistently informed by explorations of different readings of the text
AO4	consistently effective and well-developed understanding of the significance of contextual influences, such as political, theological, sociological and historical contexts

Questions and marking guidance from OCR's A Level English Literature Sample Assessment Materials

Additional questions

5 By comparing one drama and one poetry text you have studied, discuss ways in which writers make the improbable seem convincing.

6 By comparing one drama and one poetry text you have studied, discuss ways in which writers explore the temptations of power.

7 'Telle us som moral thing, that we may leere.' By comparing one drama and one poetry text you have studied, examine the ways in which writers offer moral points to their audiences.

8 By comparing one drama and one poetry text you have studied, discuss ways in which writers combine comic and serious writing in order to explore character.

AQA Specification B Section A (40 marks out of 80 in a 2-hour exam)

'The Pardoner's Tale'

Specimen question: Discuss the view that 'The Pardoner's Tale' effectively combines the macabre with a sermon on avarice.

Possible content

Candidates might consider:

- identifying elements of the 'macabre', e.g. the pursuit of Death; the nature of the sinister 'old man'
- identifying elements of the sermon, e.g. the Tale's rhetoric; its function as an illustration of the results of greed
- the ways in which the macabre elements support and inform the moralising

AQA marking guidance (Band 6: 34–40 marks)

AO1 use of appropriate critical vocabulary and technically fluent style/well-structured and coherent argument

AO1 always relevant with very sharp focus on task and confidently ranging around texts

AO2 exploration and analysis of key features of form and structure with perceptive evaluation of how they shape meanings

AO2 exploration and analysis of key aspects of form and structure with perceptive evaluation of how they shape meanings

AO3 detailed and perceptive understanding of issues raised in connecting texts through concept of Gothic/pastoral

AO3 perceptive consideration of different interpretations of texts with sharp evaluation of their strengths and weaknesses and with excellent selection of supportive references

AO4 excellent understanding of ways of contextualising Gothic/pastoral

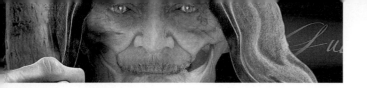

AO4   excellent understanding of a range of other contextual factors with specific, detailed links between context/text/task

Additional questions

2 How important is the character of the old man in turning a macabre story into a truly chilling one?

3 Discuss the view that, as a medieval text, 'The Pardoner's Tale' cannot be properly described as Gothic.

4 'It is the character of the Pardoner, rather than the story itself, that gives 'The Pardoner's Tale' its distinctive macabre character.' Discuss this view.

5 'It is in the corruption of religion that the text becomes horrific.' How far do you think this assessment of 'The Pardoner's Tale' is justified?

AQA Specification B Section B (40 marks out of 80 in a 2 hour exam)

Elements of the Gothic

1 'Gothic texts show the supernatural intertwined with the ordinary.' Discuss this view in relation to the texts you have been studying.

Possible content

Candidates might consider:

- what might be identified as 'supernatural' and 'ordinary' in their three chosen texts
- how such identification is open to interpretations via different cultural meanings of the key terms 'supernatural'/'Gothic'/'ordinary'
- what roles these elements play in the texts' structure
- what aspects of the texts' contextual backgrounds account for their presence
- how contemporary contexts impinge on the notion of the supernatural

2 'Gothic literature is concerned with the breaking of normal moral and social codes.' Discuss.

Possible content

Candidates might consider:

- the extent to which characters in their chosen texts illustrate actions that go against 'normal' behaviour or break boundaries set by God and/or man
- how notions of normality are cultural and so open to dispute
- the ways in which the plots enact a challenge to social convention
- the reader's response to these moral/social conflicts and possible other responses
- contextual influences, both of production and reception

3 'If a text is to be labelled as Gothic, it must convey a sense of fear and terror.' Discuss this view in relation to the texts you have been studying.

Possible content

From their three chosen texts, candidates might discuss and illustrate:

- fear/terror within the text itself and potential fear/terror for readers
- the near farcical extremes of fear/terror that Gothic sometimes has — is it frightening or is it funny?
- suspense and how it is created — and whether its impact has dimmed over time
- anticipation and chronology more generally
- delay/withholding of information: difference between reader knowledge and character knowledge
- the effect of narrative perspective and point of view
- dramatic/verbal/descriptive power
- the writer's sense of his/her audience: the possible interpretations of a contemporary readership

AQA marking guidance (Band 6: 34–40 marks)

AO1	use of appropriate critical vocabulary and technically fluent style/ well structured and coherent argument
AO1	always relevant with very sharp focus on task and confidently ranging around texts
AO2	exploration and analysis of key features of form and structure with perceptive evaluation of how they shape meanings
AO2	exploration and analysis of key aspects of form and structure with perceptive evaluation of how they shape meanings
AO3	detailed and perceptive understanding of issues raised in connecting texts through concept of Gothic/pastoral
AO3	perceptive consideration of different interpretations of texts with sharp evaluation of their strengths and weaknesses and with excellent selection of supportive references
AO4	excellent understanding of ways of contextualising Gothic/pastoral
AO4	excellent understanding of a range of other contextual factors with specific, detailed links between context/text/task

Additional questions

4 'A disturbed or twisted central character is essential for the success of a Gothic text.' Discuss how far you think this is true of the texts you have been studying.

5 'Suspense and fear are necessary components of Gothic texts.' Show how the authors develop these qualities in the texts you have been studying.

6 Consider how far it is true that Gothic texts present 'the attractiveness of the horrific'.

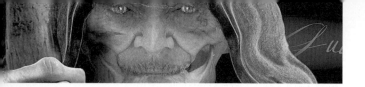

7 'The heroes of Gothic texts set themselves against God's will.' How far do you think this is true of the texts you have studied?

Main questions and marking guidance from AQA's A-level English Literature Specimen Assessment Materials

Sample essays

Below are two sample essays of different types written by different students. Both of them have been assessed as falling within the top band. You can judge them against the Assessment Objectives for this text for your exam board and decide on the exact mark you think each deserves and why. You may also be able to see ways in which each could be improved in terms of content and style.

Sample essay 1

What Gothic elements can you discover in 'The Pardoner's Prologue and Tale'?

Personally, I believe that the idea of the Gothic is best summed up in the words 'grisly' and 'macabre'. It is this which makes texts like *Frankenstein* and *Dracula* so iconic — the obsession with death and horrible violence. In this sense, 'The Pardoner's Tale' is a very successful Gothic text. 'The Pardoner's Prologue' is a rather different case, as I'll explain later.

At a superficial level 'The Pardoner's Tale' contains the basic Gothic elements. It centres on a quest for Death itself, and it features the grisly demise of the 'riotoures thre' who murder each other in hideous fashion, two of them dying with 'wonder signes of empoisoning'. Added to this there is the mysterious and macabre old man who desires 'an heyre clowt to wrappe in me', but who cannot die. Finally, there is the unchristian behaviour of the 'riotoures' who swear 'many a grisly ooth'. And I like the fact that to this character list Chaucer adds Death himself, 'that in this contree al the peple sleeth', and even the Devil, 'the feend, our enemy'.

The quest for Death is brilliantly presented, in my opinion, through the personification of Death as an active killer who 'with his spere he smoot his herte atwo' — the him being the rioters' friend, whose funeral ('a belle clinke biforn a cors') has already established aurally and visually the macabre tone of the story. The rioters instantly take up the person-ification and are grotesquely unconcerned about death: 'is it swich peril with him for to meete?' Their decision to 'sleen this false traitour' is simultaneously ridiculous and macabre. We may think the old man 'al forwrapped' is Death himself, but Chaucer has an even more effective image in the shape of the 'florins fine of gold ycoined rounde'. We can all associate the lure of money with death, and so it proves to be. Although the rioters stop looking 'lenger thanne after Deeth', we know very well they have found him, and so it is. They immediately scheme against each other, the elder to 'rive him thurgh the sides tweye', and the youngest with poison 'so strong and violent'. These brutal methods of death are characteristically Gothic.

I think that Chaucer's particular achievement is to deepen the texture of the tale by adding a Gothic mood to these macabre elements. Right at the start the revellers 'doon the devel sacrifice' with 'superfluitee abhominable' — a phrase that could come straight out of *Frankenstein*. The Pardoner adds to the mood with his rhetorical exclamations — 'O glotonye, ful of cursednesse!' He does this again after the rioters' death — 'O cursed sinne of alle cursednesse!' — so the mood is kept constant throughout. The vocabulary of the tale is always set in terms of destruction and death, particularly when Chaucer describes the behaviour of the revellers: 'Oure blessed Lordes body they totere'.

Above all there is the character of the old man, who I think casts a sinister aura over the whole tale. He is the kind of mysterious figure who is common in Gothic literature. You cannot say exactly what he is supposed to represent — that is part of the mystery — but he is always ominous and evidently symbolic. He is like a *memento mori* in medieval art; he reminds us that we are always in the presence of death, a suitably Gothic theme. The rioters meet him 'as they wolde han troden over a stile', that is to say at a point of decision. It is inevitable that they will make the wrong one, particularly when 'this olde man ful meekly hem grette', and they, young and proud and 'al drunken in this rage', merely abuse him: 'why livestow so longe'? His tapping with his 'staf, bothe erly and late', is sinister, as is the fact that he knows where Death is, 'for in that grove I lafte him, by my fey'. Unexplained, inexplicable, he darkens the atmosphere of an already dark tale.

I have concentrated on the tale that the Pardoner tells because that is where the Gothic elements are concentrated, but in a wider sense the whole of 'The Pardoner's Prologue and Tale' stands as Chaucer's venture into the Gothic mode. 'The Pardoner's Tale' is set against the character of the Pardoner himself, and he is the kind of twisted, tormented spirit that we find again and again in true Gothic literature. He has the fascination of a snake, which is apt because he compares himself to one in his prologue: 'thus spitte I out my venym'. His very soul is distorted in my opinion, and he admits it, calling himself a 'ful vicious man'. The self awareness of a doomed soul seems very modern: 'I preche of no thing but for coveitise'. I can sympathise with him to an extent, because he seems to be aware that he can do good to others even though he himself is evil: 'yet kan I maken oother folk to twynne from avarice'. However, he then repels any sympathy through his hardened attitude: 'I rekke never…though that hir soules goon a blakeberied'. Like Frankenstein's monster, our sympathy for his circumstances is in tension with our horror at the evil that he does. The Pardoner is a real Gothic creation, and this adds another layer to the complexity of the tale he tells.

Overall, then, I believe that Chaucer has succeeded in creating a very Gothic text centuries ahead of his time. What this really means, of course, is that Gothic writers like Shelley and Stoker were picking up on the grisly and macabre elements that make medieval texts like 'The Pardoner's Prologue and Tale' so striking and successful.

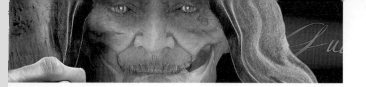

Sample essay 2

'The purpose of medieval literature was to entertain and to instruct.' Where do you think the balance lies in 'The Pardoner's Prologue and Tale'?

It is easy to see that both elements are important in 'The Pardoner's Prologue and Tale'. The portrait of the Pardoner, his confession of his own wickedness, the story he tells — all these are entertaining for the audience, but at the same time Chaucer is using them to make a moral point. It is perhaps not easy to decide exactly where 'the balance lies', so that is what this essay will attempt to discover.

The character of the Pardoner is already fully established by the time Chaucer gets to 'The Pardoner's Prologue and Tale'. The long portrait in 'The General Prologue' establishes his physical characteristics — a repelling, greasy-haired eunuch — and his moral status — a depraved, self-serving parasite on society. He is at once a memorable (and therefore entertaining) character, and a ghastly reminder of the corruption at the heart of the medieval church and medieval society. The introduction to the Pardoner's tale only confirms this impression, because he is seen as a glutton who needs a drink before he will tell a tale. The expectations of him are, frankly, not high.

Both his prologue and his tale therefore surprise the audience. The prologue is a breathtakingly brazen confession of corrupt practices, shocking and entertaining at the same time. The tale, which seems more Chaucer's than his, has the qualities of the very greatest literature — great memorability, and a real punch of a moral.

Chaucer uses comedy and irony to make the prologue amusing and effective. The Pardoner's arrogance is immediately apparent:

> And in Latin I speke a wordes fewe,
> To saffron with my predicacioun.

There is obvious contempt here for his audience, whom he expects to be impressed by his apparent learning. His delight in his own trickery is equally clear from the detailed description he gives of it:

> Lat maken with this water his potage,
> And nevere shal he moore his wif mistriste,
> Though he the soothe of hir defaute wiste,
> Al had she taken prestes two or thre.

The barbed comment at the end about priests shows him relishing his power to preach, and is highly entertaining.

However, we are aware all the time of the context in which the Pardoner is speaking. The priests he mocks are the ones whose livelihood he is taking, winning 'a hundred mark' a year. He is supposed to serve the Church, not undermine it. And he is supposed to save souls, not lead them into further sin with the promise of false pardons for unforgivable crimes like adultery. Above all there is the context of the pilgrimage which underlies *The Canterbury Tales* — if the Pardoner is not seeking his own salvation, why is he there? The answer is clear — he is on the pilgrimage to further his own cause, to sell pardons to the pilgrims themselves and anyone else he meets on the way. The depth of his depravity is revealed with his repeated claim that he does not act from disinterested motives as he should:

> For myn entente is nat but for to winne,
> And nothing for correccioun of sinne.

The Pardoner's tale takes us to a further level. The story of the three rioters is deeply satisfying on its own account. The hubris of the rioters — 'we wol sleen this false traitour Deeth' — is amply paid for in their quest for Death and its outcome. We enjoy the way that they insult the old man — 'why livestow so longe in so greet age?' — and then they fail to see that his revenge is to point them on their self-chosen road to destruction:

> 'Now, sires,' quod he, 'if that yow be so leef
> To finde Deeth, turne up this croked wey.'

The neat twist that Death appears in the form of a pile of coins is not lost on the audience, who again enjoy the rioters' blindness about this obvious fact. And their mutual murders are a neat and satisfying denouement.

Again, we can enjoy this story for itself. But Chaucer offers us two layers of meaning. Firstly, the tale is a moral tale. It is a story about sin and the consequences of sin — 'the wages of sin is death', as the Bible says. Even if we are not Christians, we can appreciate the powerful moral points about behaviour, about arrogance, about betrayal. But to this Chaucer adds the second contextual level of its relationship to the teller, the Pardoner. The fact that this moral tale is narrated by a character who is, to borrow his own phrase, 'moost envoluped in sinne', doubles its effect, because the Pardoner, like the rioters, is a blasphemer who faces eternal damnation for his sins. Just as the rioters should turn from the 'croked wey' into the straight way of the Lord, so should the Pardoner. He, like them, is seemingly blind to his own danger. His blatant attempt to dupe the pilgrims at the end, despite having confessed his own falseness to them, can be seen as an exact parallel to the rioters' failure to understand their own circumstances. The Pardoner warns of the dangers of dying without repentance:

> Peraventure ther may fallen oon or two
> Doun of his hors, and breke his nekke atwo,

and yet seems oblivious to his own doom.

In conclusion, it is safe to say that there is a complete balance between the entertainment and the moralistic elements of 'The Pardoner's Prologue and Tale', as much for a modern audience as, presumably, for Chaucer's own.

Further study

Editions

The standard edition is now *The Riverside Chaucer* (general editor, Larry D. Benson, Oxford University Press, 3rd edn., 2008).

Modernised versions

Strictly speaking, it is wrong to use the word 'translation' for Chaucer, as his work (like Shakespeare's) is written in English, albeit Middle English. These are really modernisations, but the word 'translation' is often used.

The best known are the verse renderings by Nevill Coghill (Penguin) and David Wright (Oxford World's Classics). While these give a flavour of Chaucer for the non-specialist, a prose version is more suitable for studying, because it allows direct comparison with the original text. The recommended work is David Wright's prose modernisation of *The Canterbury Tales* (Fontana, 1996). Although not currently in print it can easily be acquired second-hand. It omits the 'Tale of Melibee' and 'The Parson's Tale', but is otherwise the best way to read the complete *Tales*.

Readings

The easiest way to hear Chaucer's work read aloud is via the internet; there are a number of sites that offer extracts or complete tales, and some give pronunciation guides too. See the section on internet resources below. Libraries may have audio CD versions.

Background reading

There is a daunting number of books on Chaucer available; your school and local library will have a selection. It is worth looking out for the following:

- Brewer, D. (1996) *Chaucer and His World*, Eyre Methuen. This is an excellent visual and biographical account of Chaucer. Derek Brewer has written and edited a number of accessible books on Chaucer.
- Burrow, J. (1982) *Medieval Writers and Their Work: Middle English Literature and its Background 1100–1500*, Oxford University Press. This study places Chaucer in his literary context.
- Gray, D. (ed.) (2003) *The Oxford Companion to Chaucer*, Oxford University Press. This major volume amounts to a complete encyclopedia of Chaucer and contains over 2,000 entries.
- Rowland, B. (ed.) (1979) *Companion to Chaucer Studies*, Oxford University Press. This contains useful essays on allegory and irony, and other essays on Chaucer and his background.

The internet

The internet is a marvellous source of material on Chaucer, because it permits the use of illustrations and sound in a way that not even the best books can match. There is also an enormous quantity of up-to-date material available, ranging from student guides to academic studies. A good search engine (Google is recommended) and the willingness to spend some time exploring will reveal considerable riches, and often unexpected and useful insights into all aspects of Chaucer's works, period and culture. The following are excellent starting points:

- www.unc.edu/depts/chaucer/ is the *Chaucer Metapage* and should be the first port of call. It is designed to act as a guide to Chaucer resources on the internet.
- www.kankedort.net/ contains *The Electronic Canterbury Tales* and a wealth of other information.
- www.mathomtrove.org/canterbury/links.htm is an excellent page of links to material on Chaucer and on the medieval background.
- www.courses.fas.harvard.edu/~chaucer/index.html includes an interactive guide to Chaucer's pronunciation, grammar and vocabulary, and interlinear modernisations of some of the tales.
- www.gutenberg.org/wiki/Main_Page is the home page of Project Gutenberg, which exists to provide the texts of copyright-free material from all eras.
- www.lib.rochester.edu/camelot/teams/tmsmenu.htm is the home page of The Consortium for the Teaching of the Middle Ages, and has introductions to and the texts of hundreds of medieval works.
- www.unc.edu/depts/chaucer/zatta/Zatta_Index.html is Jane Zatta's site for *The Canterbury Tales*. There is first-rate material on the Pardoner at www.unc.edu/depts/chaucer/zatta/pardoner.html
- www.fordham.edu/halsall/sbook.html is the home of the *Internet Medieval Sourcebook*. This is a huge resource of medieval sources and texts, including for example information on pilgrimages, saints and relics.
- www.librarius.com/cantlink/pardonlk.htm has useful further resources, information and essays.
- http://humanities.byu.edu/rhetoric/silva.htm is a site called *The Forest of Rhetoric*, a comprehensive guide to rhetoric with explanations of all the terms.
- http://www.luminarium.org/medlit/chaucessays.htm has links to a range of essays about the Pardoner.
- www.luc.edu/publications/medieval/vol3/hicks.html has an essay entitled 'Chaucer's Inversion of Augustinian Rhetoric in the Pardoner's Prologue and Tale' by James E. Hicks.
- www.stjohns-chs.org/english/Medieval/pdr.html includes the text of G. L. Kittredge's seminal 1893 essay on the Pardoner, which is still worth consideration although much of its argument has been superseded in later criticism.

- www.encyclopedia.com/doc/1E1-relics.html has a useful note about the modern status of relics in the Roman Catholic Church.
- http://stjudeshrine.org.uk/reltext.htm has a further modern perspective on relics, written by the Carmelite Fr. Christopher O'Donnell.